I0180060

*"I see this book as very relevant to the youth as a training manual."*
—Chris Piper, Director of Operations, Don Piper Ministries.

*"[It is] refreshing to see a call to personal holiness by Mr. Hignight's book ... actually engage in spiritual warfare, and we shall see far more victory than if we sit on the sidelines."*
—Dr. Ronald Shultz, Pastor

*"With a friendly 'big-brother-who's-been-there' style, author Randy Hignight challenges us to attain a life that is pleasing to God ... a fantastic resource for new believers and old-timers alike—so we can all grow in Christ and enjoy total victory!"*
—Shari Lacey, Radical Recovery Ministries

*"Hignight's book is motivating and enlightening, to say the least. His 'total victory perspective' is predicated on personal holiness. His call to holiness is actually a call to spiritual warfare while avoiding temptation and sin by entering into prayer, spiritual combat, and praise."*
—Jerry Perry, Newspaper Lifestyles Editor

*"I'm fourteen years old. I am writing to you about your book,* BIG GOD little problem. *This book is one of the greatest Christian books I have ever read. I love how the book tells and shows verses in the Bible to show and prove that what you are saying helps others in their walk with God. I strongly recommend this book."*
—Daniel

*"[This book] simplifies things in a complex world, renewed by thinking about spiritual warfare and how to STOP at temptation."*
—Robert Martinez

BIG GOD
LITTLE PROBLEM
"Behold, I am the LORD, the God of all flesh;
is there any thing too hard for me?"
Jeremiah 32:27
RANDY HIGNIGHT

Laurus Books

# BIG GOD

## LITTLE PROBLEM

by Randy Hignight, Sr.



Paperback: ISBN: 978-1-938526-86-2

Mobi (Kindle): ISBN: 978-1-938526-87-9

ePub (iBooks, Nook): ISBN: 978-1-938526-88-6

Published by Laurus Books

Printed in the United States of America

Cover design by Brittany Darr

Laurus Books
P.O. Box 530173
DeBary, FL 32753-0173 USA
www.TheLaurusCompany.com

This book may be ordered in paperback from TheLaurusCompany.com, Amazon.com, BarnesandNoble.com, and other retailers around the world. Also available in formats for electronic readers from their respective stores. Please contact publisher for quantity purchases.

This book is dedicated to
God the Father, Jesus the Son, and the Holy Spirit,
without Whom I would never, ever have been able
to write this offering at all.
Thank You, LORD!

I also dedicate this book to
my wife, Bobbette,
my son, Randy, Jr., and
my daughter, Brittany.
I love you!

# TABLE OF CONTENTS

# TABLE OF CONTENTS CONT.

# ACKNOWLEDGEMENTS

## Thank You!

I want to thank my family for their support throughout the years of testing that the Lord allowed, which got me to the point of completing this writing.

Special thanks to Brittany Darr for the cover design. Brittany can be reached at darrlingdesign@aol.com.

Thank you to A'Ree Hunt and Angie Roden for the time you put into proofreading and formatting the original manuscript.

Thanks to Mark Nelson for his input in the creation of the original work on this book. Mark is an accomplished photographer and can be contacted at www.markanthonynelson.com.

Thanks to Jorge Arbelaez for the Total Victory Perspective (TVP) logo design. Contact Jorge for all kinds of graphic designs, illustrations, and multimedia at www.arturastudios.com.

Thank you to Jerry Bell for the wonderful artwork throughout the book. Jerry has been an artist for over 30 years, illustrating and designing cartoons to T-shirts and everything in between. Contact Jerry to create something fantastic at liberty_creations@yahoo.com.

Last but not least, I wish to thank my editor, Nancy E. Williams with Laurus Books, for the design and editing of the final edition of this book. I love her improvements. Contact Nancy at www.TheLaurusCompany.com.

I hope I left no one out in listing my appreciation for support. To all of you who may not be listed, you know I love you and truly appreciate your prayers and conversations with me along the way. Thank you.

# FOREWORD

*"Be strong and of good courage, do not fear nor be afraid of them;*
*for the LORD your God, He is the One who goes with you.*
*He will not leave you nor forsake you."*
Deuteronomy 31:6

I want to tell you that when I wrote my first book, I had no idea of the trial I would face after the book was out in its fourth year. The project launched, and people's lives were being impacted by the message. I went to book signings and was able to guest speak on several occasions. I really was humbled that I was allowed to go through a fire in the supernatural realm that allowed me to write such a powerfully freeing message. I was moving forward and was also involved in a music project. My song, "Freedom Your Freedom," brought awareness to people that the military deserves honor and that someone dies each day to keep us safe. (There is an NBC special on YouTube under my name.)

I was busy speaking, singing, and writing when, I was suddenly struck with cancer. I had surgery, and they were able to get it all. I am so grateful that God spared my life. At the time of this writing, I have been cancer free for over two years.

## A NEW COVER AND TITLE

After my recovery from cancer surgery, my publisher and I decided to make some changes to my book, with a new cover design and a new title. I prayed and asked the Lord what the new title should be. After a while, I was impressed to call it "Big God little problem." I asked the Lord what this title was about? He is our BIG GOD, and the problems we have are little when we consider His plan. God loves us and has our best interest in mind. So, what is the little problem in the world? Are you ready for the answer? The little problem in the world is Satan. There is no power struggle between God and Satan. Devils are a little problem when we give our lives over to the Creator of all things, the Mighty Lord.

At one time, I did not know these things. I was overrun by deception for many years. My hope is that you will catch hold of that which took me years of personal failure to learn. Receive the truth and live each day in the victory of Christ.

Before the new book was completed, my publisher and friend, Nancy Williams, had to have emergency surgery. She was in sepsis when she went to the ER, and the surgeon said she would probably have died if the infection had gone one more day. So cancer tried to get me, and the enemy was trying to kill Nancy before this new book got launched. We know, however, that our God is bigger than any of the devil's schemes. *"What shall we then say to these things? If God be for us, who can be against us?"* (Romans 8:31)..

## BONDAGE TO SEX

At the time of this release, I am working on another book about my ancestry and the sexual immorality that was rampant in my family, from my great-grandfather of Choctaw descent all the way down to me. My father left me when I was two years old. He was a gang member and a pimp. I met him again when I was fourteen years old. At that time, he was a very wealthy man and gave me cars and motorcycles. He even gave me access to his boat. I was a very immoral young man. I got married at age nineteen and practiced adultery for over eight years after marriage until God intervened and set me free.

While I was trying to decide whether to reveal the details of my past, my publisher reminded me, "God has spared your life for a reason. This story needs to be told because so many others suffer with the same affliction." The forthcoming book will have chapter titles such as *Why Not Pornography, Satan Attends Church, The Mind of An Adulterer, Sex Approved by God,* along with a lot of spiritual warfare training. The book will be coming out in late 2015, and the projected title is *Sex God's Way*.

This book you are holding is a precursor to the *Sex God's Way* book. This book lays the foundation for freedom from any kind of sinful temptation.

Right now, let me encourage you that someone needs you. Someone is going through a trial, perhaps a trial of temptation or possibly even a cancer trial, or their family is. I exhort you to reach out to them, buy them a gift card, give them cash, take them to dinner, whatever you feel led to do, but please do something for them. I remember how much it touched me that relatives and friends cared, and I remember also how hurt I was that so many did not. Please reach out to the people in your realm who are having a tough time in a trial of sickness or the loss of a loved one. Don't hesitate; go and show the love of God.

> You can be the one now.
> You can go the distance.
> You can cause the changes.
> You can make a difference.

— Randy Hignight

# PREFACE

*"Behold, I am the LORD, the God of all flesh:*
*is there any thing too hard for Me?"*
Jeremiah 32:27

Whatever problem you are dealing with, WELCOME to VICTORY IN CHRIST!

**Big God little problem**

What is the end objective? We believe it is holiness, or maturity in Christ. I pray that you take the teaching of God's Word being presented here and apply it immediately. Dedicate your life, and strive not to fail. STUDY HIS WORD! Go to church. Pray for the believers and for the lost. Each day when you wake up, choose to obey the Lord, and ask Him to show you the way. He will supply all the power and direction you need to be the servant He wants you to be. Live in His purity from now on.

I wrote this book to wake you up, so that you would not be deceived. Please do not be deceived any longer. Now is your opportunity to decide. You can strive to live a holy life or keep doing what you have been doing.

Ask Jesus what He wants from you, and go into the world and preach the gospel of POWER. The REAL power He gave us is here to show the world. Time is passing by, and more souls are in need of a Savior. Now GO!

God bless you, in Jesus' name.

—Randy Hignight, Sr.

# MY STATEMENT OF FAITH

After many years of praying and serving the Lord, I felt led to write a statement of how I wanted to live my life unto God. I wrote down and signed the statement of faith to the Lord in December 1998. I then signed my name to it.

The copy of what I actually wrote is shown below. It is still wonderful to look back at the statement I made all those years ago. I had no idea what all the future was to hold. It was the next year in November of 1999 when the Lord allowed me to undergo pressure-packed demonic testing that lasted five years. The test was extreme, but I trusted God was going to deliver me, and He did! The final result of the test allowed me the insight to write this book and give the world the option to choose Total Victory Perspective (TVP).

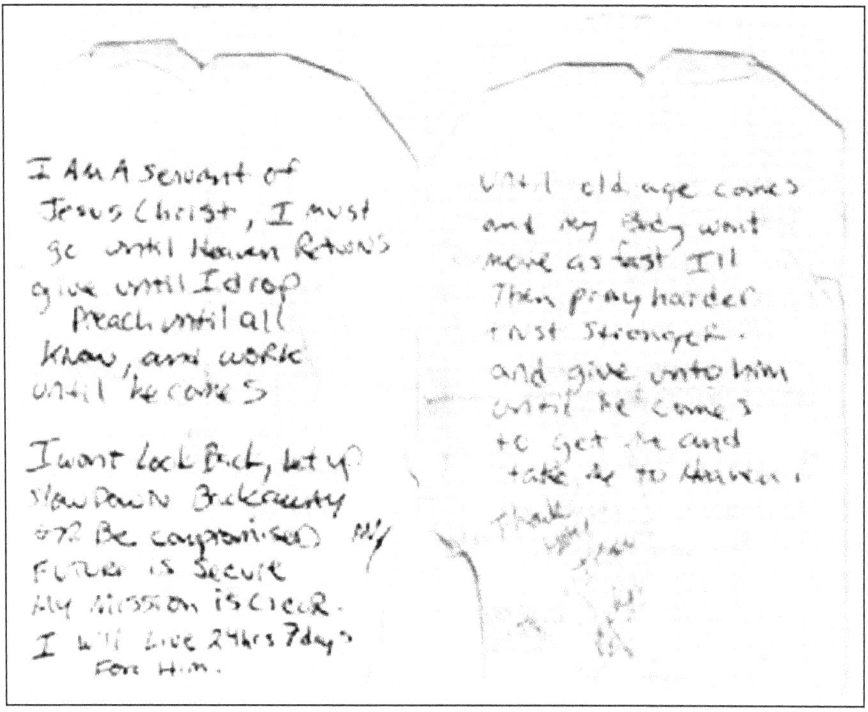


DISCLAIMER: In the final edit of this book before going to print, I discovered a similarity in my statement of faith to a couple of lines in a poem by Dr. Bob Moorehead titled "The Fellowship of the Unashamed." Although my statement of faith was similar to what Dr. Moorehead wrote, it was written 10 years prior to reading anything from this pastor.

# YOUR STATEMENT OF FAITH

Below, you will find space to write down your own statement to God. Years from now, you can look back at the statement you wrote and see what has happened in your life. You will see how God worked in your life to grow you and fulfill your statement. Pray and read over this book, then come back, fill it in, and sign your own personal note if you desire.

Please read this book first, as your perspective may change. Then come back and write your note to God. Be sure to sign it.

Signature

Date

# Introducing ...

## The Need-To-Know Guy

**Whenever you see him in this book, PLEASE PAY ATTENTION! He will be pointing you to a verse or verses you NEED TO KNOW that will direct you to personal VICTORY every time!**

**TOTAL VICTORY PERSPECTIVE:** *Learn it, live it, share it!*™

# PART 1

## CHOOSE NOT TO SIN

# CHAPTER 1

## Urgent Subject Matter

This book is written for the disturbing number of people in the world who say they want to obey God but continue to fail. I believe the Lord's Word will point the person who wants to obey God to the means to success. Please bear with me for a little while.

What if a Christian could be boosted to a stronger stance against the supernatural realm of evil? How compelling would it be for a Christian to have a testimony of truly holy living? That kind of witness would be so evident that no one could deny an extreme difference.

Those who do not understand think I am saying that you cannot sin after you have received Christ as your Savior. This is a misunderstanding of what I am teaching. A Christian certainly can sin, but I urge believers to use every Scripture to learn how to stop temptation before it becomes action.

You have a free choice to stop at temptation by utilizing God's power. It will take commitment and a lot of work to stop at temptation and take captive every thought. Yes, it is hard, but not impossible! Would you be interested in considering a few Scriptures that will help you? Jesus is the Way, and He has the final Word. Are you ready to boost your walk with the Lord?

Up front, please allow me to set the record straight. My understanding of *holy* is "pure, perfect, without sin," not "you are not able to sin." If you decide to take your free choice, you, a believer in Christ, can stop at temptation. It will take a lot of personal effort to recognize and stop before sinning, but it is not impossible!

> *"For he chose us in him before the creation of the world to be holy and blameless in his sight."* (Ephesians 1:4)

> *"Be perfect, therefore, as your heavenly Father is perfect."* (Matthew 5:48)

Later, I will share with you three Bible passages that I have re-evaluated. I would like you to see the Scripture usage in what I have come to call "Total Victory Perspective" (TVP). I have searched deeply in the Scriptures and held my ground to serve God in holiness despite demon attacks. Satan may say, "Don't make the Christian realm simple; people might understand." But being a Christian *can* be simple. I have withstood some torment over my stand and, with the Lord's help, emerged victorious.

The Lord settled me and soothed me for a season, and then asked, "Do you trust Me?"

I said, "Yes."

He said, "Let's go!"

The Lord took me through a personal five-year training course. He allowed me to hear and feel things from the demonic realm like never before! Maybe some day I will explain more in depth, either in another book or as a guest speaker, what all was allowed into my realm to train me. But the focus of this book is not about me. I want to amplify Jesus. He is the answer for all things!

Since that time, the Lord has enabled me to live in unshakable spiritual warfare against the enemy, understanding all by the power of God's Word. I would like to condense what I learned to a fast track to holy living for today's Christian! Perhaps you can be spared some of the hard lessons.

I kept reading the Scriptures and praying continually, "Lord, is it really that simple? This training You gave me is extremely powerful but really simple. Lord, this is Your business. What do You want me to do with this information?"

I heard the Spirit speak, "I will set your appointments."

A powerful perspective has been revealed to me called:

**"Total Victory Perspective To Holy Living"**

Are you interested in serving the Lord with all your heart, soul, and strength? Do you desire to please Him by being holy in all your conduct? Then read on!

Jesus paid the price and reversed the curse for those who receive Him by faith! Really, He did! It is finished! God's power is all we ever need to succeed and live a pure life. Your total devotion means asking all things of the Lord, every minute of the day.

I really believe Christians are making it too hard to serve the Lord. It is going to be a slow process to lovingly take the Christian community by the hand and lead it back to the original power.

God is holy, and His mercy endures forever. He sent His Son to pay the penalty for sin, and now it is finished!

God does expect you to be perfect (holy), but God does not expect perfection. "What?" you ask. Perfection would be selfish ambition, which is a sin that was crucified in Christ. Perfection drives you to have things your way. Perfection induces pride and glorifies self. It can even cause you to become contentious in certain situations.

Perfection is about not making mistakes. Holiness is about not committing sins. We need to know the difference between *mistakes* and *sin*. A mistake is leaving a pizza in the oven too long, or sawing a board the wrong length, or cutting a piece of material crooked. Sin has to do with rebellion and willful wrong choices. Do not be a perfectionist (selfish ambition), but be perfect (holy)! Do you see the difference? Perfect, but not perfection!

# You Need To Know ...

## What God Expects

*"But just as he who called you is holy, so be holy in all you do; for it is written: 'Be holy, because I am holy.' "* (1 Peter 1:15-16)

*"Be perfect, therefore, as your heavenly Father is perfect."* (Matthew 5:48)

**TOTAL VICTORY PERSPECTIVE:** ***Learn it, live it, share it!***™

# CHAPTER 2

# Mind-Bending Information

*"Be perfect, therefore, as your heavenly Father is perfect."*
(Matthew 5:48)

The Scriptures have come alive with a renewed meaning of the power that Jesus gives! After intense study of the Scriptures, I see a slight difference from what I was taught about temptation and sin. This knowledge has changed my life!

I practice what I have learned, and the results are wonderful! My own family has been trained in this information, and my son and daughter are living pure lives unto the Lord. The training works! Jesus really is the final Word for all things.

Through the years, long before I wrote this book, I was handing out papers with lists of Scriptures and pointing out how to understand spiritual warfare. I would stop teens at church and ask about their walk with the Lord. Occasionally, I would teach them Scriptures to commit to memory for a better understanding of spiritual warfare. I have trained a few young men in spiritual warfare without knowing it was going to be called "TVP" in the future. I know it is a mind-bender to accept the perspective that we are really now complete in Christ! The years have gone by, and those young boys are now grown men living for the Lord.

One young man named Trenton Wheeler has become a great man of God. He was a music leader and formed his own Christian band to perform at various events for the glory of the Lord. He lives the holy life and is a great example of a believer's free choice and God's power to direct a young man into adulthood with purity.

**Total Victory Perspective** teaching is producing strong Christians. Individuals in Christ can recognize temptation and utilize the power in Jesus to combat sin.

I asked the Lord if it was okay to take the information and insight He gave me to His people. I said, "Lord, this information is mind-bending and extreme in how it differs from what is now being taught."

It has taken me years to put this writing together, but the bottom line is reflected in results: I have witnessed several people whose lives, at best, were mediocre in the Lord who are now living a stronger Christian life each and every day. That is a testimony to the world of holy living.

# CHAPTER 3
# Lack of Knowledge

*"... my people are destroyed from lack of knowledge."*
(Hosea 4:6)

God's people can seek the knowledge of His Word and live each moment of this life in victory over all darkness, seen or unseen.

Do you choose to obey God? If your answer is yes, you have made the correct decision, and God has already provided the way. Nothing can keep you from serving and obeying. Nothing!

Or is there something? Don't flip out, but we are about to embark on a journey into the spiritual world of the devil and his angels. Buckle up because it is a rough ride ahead. Jesus Christ, however, is more powerful than the devil's deception. The Bible gives us direction for pure living, so let's go!

The Lord revealed to me that we must rethink the day. Most Christians say (by their actions), "The day is long. I know I will sin today." You sleep eight hours or more and are awake sixteen hours. Is it possible to focus 16 times a day on not failing to stop a temptation? What about 32 times a day—every 30 minutes? Can you keep in touch with the Lord in order not to sin? Will it take 64 times a day—every 15 minutes—for you to ask the Lord to get you out of trouble before you sin? Hopefully, you get the idea. We have twenty-four hours a day and free choice every minute of that day. Let's use our free choice to recognize temptation and choose not to sin. We have free choice, right? Then choose! God set you free from sin. He sent His Son to free you from sin, not for you to fail Him.

I believe that once we receive God's salvation, we are merely tempted by an unseen fallen angel. Even if it takes every seven seconds of your day to focus on stopping at the temptation and using the Word of God to not sin, you can do it! I have been doing it every day for years. If I can do it, you can do it!

**FIRST SIN AND THE RESULT ...**

# You Need To Know ...

## The First Sin and God's Reaction

*"And there was war in heaven. Michael and his angels fought against the dragon, and the dragon and his angels fought back. But he was not strong enough, and they lost their place in heaven. The great dragon was hurled down – that ancient serpent called the devil, or Satan, who leads the whole world astray. He was hurled to the earth, and his angels with him." (Revelation 12:7-9)*

**TOTAL VICTORY PERSPECTIVE:** ***Learn it, live it, share it!***™

# CHAPTER 4

# Advanced Training

After reading this book, a person should have a greater understanding of:

- why Jesus came to earth,
- what happened in heaven with Lucifer,
- where all the disobedient, condemned devils go,
- where the devils and angels are now, and
- where the final stop is for all disobedient spirits.

We will also explore why the Lord allows devils to attack His serving believers. (It's only a spiritual tune-up for your benefit; don't be scared.)

Too much talk about devils? The Christian realm is being crushed by divorce, drugs, immorality, and whatever else is disobedience to God. We should be seeking everything possible in God's Word to find out how to live in righteousness and stop failing.

Just because the devils cannot be seen does not mean they are not there. A corporeal Jesus cannot be seen, yet when asked into the heart of a free-choice creation, there is no doubt of His presence. The point is that we are all part of a spiritual existence. Look at the world around us. You will see hatred, greed, immorality, and destruction in Christian lives. If we are supposed to be the "light" of the world, then what is going on? Christians are doing what the world is doing! How can this be, when all the power of God has been given to all who believe on His Son?

There are some rules to the game, and if you know them, then you will have the victory every time! (God put the rules in the Bible for us to know exactly how to be victorious.)

> *"Similarly, if anyone competes as an athlete, he does not receive the victor's crown unless he competes according to the rules."* (2 Timothy 2:5)

## SOME OF THE BOTTOM LINE RULES

1. God is holy—you must be the same to be on His team.
2. The first disobedience was in heaven—Satan and the fallen angels.
3. The second disobedience was in the Garden of Eden—Adam disobeyed God and sin entered the world.
4. A price had to be paid for the sin—the one-time pure sacrifice of God's Son.
5. Free choice—you have a free choice to accept or reject God.
6. God accepts the bloodshed of His Holy Son as your payment for sin.
7. Receive Jesus as your Savior and you are given the Holy Spirit.
8. Free choice after receiving Jesus allows you His power to say no to sin every time, if you choose.
9. You will be tempted, but temptation is not sin. Do not give in to sin; you are now holy.
10. Anyone who has received Christ as Savior is sealed for eternal life, and a pure life can be lived at any spiritual level.

> *"For God so loved the world that he gave his one and only Son, that whoever believes in him shall not perish but have eternal life."* (John 3:16)

> *"... but as He who called you is holy, you also be holy in all your conduct, because it is written, 'Be holy, for I am holy.'"* (1 Peter 1:15-16 NKJV)

Are you ready for the top level of service? We should all be seeking to grow in our service to the Lord Almighty.

## THE DECISION IS CLEAR. THE POWER IS YOURS.

## WHAT DO YOU SEE?

*"His tail swept a third of the stars out of the sky and flung them to the earth. The dragon stood in front of the woman who was about to give birth, so that he might devour her child the moment it was born."* (Revelation 12:4)

# CHAPTER 5

# God's Reaction To Sin

*"... be holy in all your conduct ... 'Be holy, for I am holy.'"*
(1 Peter 1:15-16 NKJV)

As far as I can see, God wants us to always be holy (pure, no sin). God takes sin very seriously as you will see in the following accounts:

- Lucifer's one sin resulted in his being cast out of heaven with one-third of the angels.
- Adam's one sin resulted in Adam and Eve being removed from the Garden of Eden, and the world was turned over to sin.
- God flooded the whole world in judgment of sin but saved Noah and his family in the ark he had built.
- God sent fire and brimstone down to destroy the sinful cities of Sodom and Gomorrah.
- God immediately struck down Ananias and Sapphira for lying to the Holy Spirit one time!

Again, as far as I can see, God wants us to always be holy. He did not have Jesus suffer and die on the cross to make sin an acceptable practice. We don't get saved so we can keep on sinning without penalty. Sin has consequences even if you are a Christian. Sometimes they are natural consequences, such as the child who gets hurt after disobeying his parents.

What I am saying is, rather than having to repent again and again or suffer consequences for our willful sins, let's focus on not sinning. Stop, use the power of God's Word before you give in to sin. If you sin, you can repent. I suggest that you repent quickly and recognize what is going on. Ask the Lord to allow you not to be deceived into sin the next time you are tempted.

> *"My little children, these things I write to you, so that you may not sin. And if anyone sins, we have an Advocate with the Father, Jesus Christ the righteous."* (1 John 2:1 NKJV)

Jesus came to remove something that God hates: SIN. Sin is not acceptable to the Lord. He has always been against sin!

In John 8 (NKJV), Jesus told the woman who was brought to Him after being caught in the middle of adultery, "... go and sin no more."

Then Jesus said in Matthew 5:48, "Be perfect, therefore, as your heavenly Father is perfect."

These words came before He went to the cross and crucified the sin of the world. Notice He does not say to the woman, "Try hard ..." Nor did He say to the people, "... be so-so." He adamantly said, "Be perfect." *Holy* is what God expects, but the sin penalty price had to be paid. JESUS paid it. *It is finished!* Thank you, Jesus!

**ONE SIN, AND ADAM AND EVE WERE REMOVED FROM THE HOLY GARDEN!**

# You Need To Know...

## God Gave Adam the Rules Up Front

*"And the Lord God commanded the man, 'You are free to eat from any tree in the garden; but you must not eat from the tree of the knowledge of good and evil, for when you eat of it you will surely die.'" (Genesis 2:16-17)*

Read Genesis 1 through 3, and notice how exactly God instructs Adam!

**TOTAL VICTORY PERSPECTIVE:** ***Learn it, live it, share it!™***

# CHAPTER 6

## Sin Visual Aid on 3x5 Cards

I was driving down the road one night, and the Lord revealed to me how He views sin and gave me a visual aid to use to show others. This is how it goes.

Take some 3x5 cards and write "SIN" on the top of each one. Flip the cards over, and write down the name of a particular sin on each one, such as adultery, hatred, murder, envy, illegal drugs, witchcraft, outbursts of wrath, lying, and so on. One side of your card will say "SIN," and when you flip it over, the other side will be an actual named sin.

Now turn all the cards over where you can see only the side marked "SIN." The Lord spoke to me and said, "This is how I feel about sin. I hate all sins and crucified them all." As He looks across the cards, He sees sin as total and complete disobedience, and He sees the price that had to be paid by the blood of Jesus to cleanse all who will call on His name. The Lord said to me that we are not calling sin what it is. We flip one card over, and if we feel that particular act is somehow not as bad a sin as something else, we justify it. We are rating sin instead of seeing it for the evil that it is. God hates all sin, and Jesus died for the sin of the world to free us from the devil's lies.

Flip one card over. It says "HATRED" on the other side, and we say that it is not nice to hate. "Yes, Jesus wants us to love, but that person really makes me mad. I'm only human, so I will hold this hatred. After all, he did me wrong."

Flip over another card, and it says "DRUG ADDICTION." We say, "Oh, that sin is worse because it's dangerous. We will pray for people like that, but let's keep our distance from someone who is or has ever been that way."

The next card we flip over says "MURDER," and we say, "Whoa, that is too heavy. I don't want to forgive someone who did something like that. I would never murder anyone. No, that sin is too heavy."

Now flip over the card that says "OUTBURSTS OF WRATH," and we say, "There are a lot of Christians who scream and carry on in traffic or at home with the spouse or the kids. It's normal." We judge yelling as a small thing, but it's not small to God.

You see how the 3x5 card insight works? Now, share it with others. It is an eye-opening visual tool to show the games that devils play to deceive us into believing some sins are not as bad as others. God deals seriously with all sin. Let's stop rating sin and justifying it on some personal scale.

We may feel sure that God will understand and not judge certain sins as harshly, but devils are slippery at what they do. They are deceiving believers into thinking about sin in categories. "Pick out how you feel about sin," the devils will say. "Yes, there are the easy-to-swallow small sins and the medium sins—*not as bad as those other people*. And then there are the vile, sick, twisted sins."

We say to ourselves that we are so glad we only sin a little, not like those evil sinners. "We can never be perfect, so why try too hard?"

It's not that devils do not attack a believer, it's the constant, relentlessness of their attacks; the believer becomes unable to discern what a satanic attack really is.

Let's take a minute to pray …

> *Thank You, Father God, for sending us Your Son. Thank You, Jesus, for the price that You have paid. I praise Your wonderful name! Thank You for Your gift. Praise be to You, Lord! Thank You for giving us Your Holy Spirit. Thank You, Lord, thank You. What a great price You have paid to crucify sin. Lord, we, Your creation, love You and desire to serve You. Lead us by Your Spirit, Lord. We choose to obey. Thank You for allowing us the right to worship and praise You. You alone are worthy of all praise and honor, for there is no other name above the name of Jesus. Amen.*

# CHAPTER 7

## Born Again

"Saved" is a Christian word we often sling around. We ask, "Are you saved?" Do we really understand the word, or is it being used without thought?

If Adam had not sinned, we would not need to be saved. With God, no one gets away with anything, and a future wrath is coming. So when we ask someone if they are "saved," we are asking if they are saved from the wrath of God to come.

If you have repented from sin and asked Jesus into your heart, you are saved, and God sends His Holy Spirit to seal you. The truth is, the experience is supernatural, and you are born again out of the world and into the ownership of Jesus Christ.

Let's spend a moment discussing this phrase, "born again." Everyone is born naturally into the world in the first birth. This is called being born "of water." The natural birth carries with it the curse of sin that came when Adam disobeyed God in the Garden of Eden. Because of Adam's disobedience, sin entered the world. Everyone born since Adam's sin is born with the sin nature. This sin nature is opposed to God. That one act of disobedience in the Garden caused the whole world to be turned over to sin.

> *"Therefore, just as through one man sin entered the world, and death through sin, and thus death spread to all men, because all sinned ..."* (Romans 5:12 NKJV).

So, according to the Bible, the first birth leaves everyone falling into the same category. *"... for all have sinned and fall short of the glory of God ..."* (Romans 3:23 NKJV).

Jesus declared to a man named Nicodemus, *"I tell you the truth, no one can see the kingdom of God unless he is born again"* (John 3:3).

Being born of water into the world brings by inheritance the same sin condition of the whole world. God is holy, so to have righteousness (a right standing with God), you have to be holy. But Jesus said, "You must be born again." If you want to be in right standing with God while on this earth and to be with God after the last breath of life, you must have a supernatural, spiritual rebirth. You must move from the first birth (born of water with a sin nature from the disobedience in the garden) to the second birth (born of spirit, accepting God's gift, His only Son). Rebirth occurs when you receive Jesus as your Savior because He is the only One who took on the sin of the world and crucified it. If you receive Jesus as your Lord, He will then give you the Holy Spirit. Once you have been given the Spirit of God, you are no longer under the condemnation of sin. The old is gone. When you receive the Spirit of God, you are truly born again.

> *"Therefore, if anyone is in Christ, he is a new creation; the old has gone, the new has come!"* (2 Corinthians 5:17)

> *"Those who belong to Christ Jesus have crucified the sinful nature with its passions and desires."* (Galatians 5:24)

Many people experience an emotional high when they receive Jesus! The born-again emotional high does not usually last very long. Your personal life intervenes and the born-again "feeling" diminishes. What now? You are saved, but it feels like Jesus has left you adrift.

Some people get saved and are fired up emotionally from that day forward, but most people, including myself, have a short-lived "saved feeling." Yet, God said, "Never will I leave you; never will I forsake you" (Hebrews 13:5).

The initial experience of being born again is wonderful, but what do you do when you don't feel as close to the Lord as you first did? It's time to put down the baby bottle and get hold of a knife and fork. Get ready to eat the beef, the meat of God's Word. Are you ready?

Your life is very short, even if you live to 120 years. Most people live a lot less time than that. God knows your days, and He has a plan laid out for you, a plan to live a pure and blameless life.

> *"For he chose us in him before the creation of the world to be holy and blameless in his sight."* (Ephesians 1:4)

> *"For though by this time you ought to be teachers, you need someone to teach you again the first principles of the oracles of God; and you have come to need milk and not solid food. For everyone who partakes only of milk is unskilled in the word of righteousness, for he is a babe. But solid food belongs to those who are of full age, that is, those who by reason of use have their senses exercised to discern both good and evil."* (Hebrews 5:12-14 NKJV)

# You Need To Know ...

## When Adam sinned, God removed him and his wife from the Garden - No Compromise!

*"To Adam he said, 'Because you listened to your wife and ate from the tree about which I commanded you, 'You must not eat of it,' cursed is the ground because of you; through painful toil you will eat of it all the days of your life. So the Lord God banished him from the Garden of Eden to work the ground from which he had been taken. After he drove the man out, he placed on the east side of the Garden of Eden cherubim and a flaming sword flashing back and forth to guard the way to the tree of life."* (Genesis 3:17, 23-24)

**TOTAL VICTORY PERSPECTIVE:** ***Learn it, live it, share it!***™

NOTE: Adam's sin was the second sin committed by God's created beings. The first sin was Lucifer's rebellion in heaven. See page 23.

# CHAPTER 8

# What Things Happened at the Fall of Man?

**Everything** was changed **forever** at the fall of man! When Adam disobeyed, the holy connection with God was broken and many things were affected. Even the ground was cursed.

God loves His creation, and He put into motion a plan guaranteeing reconciliation for those who would accept it. The cost was going to be enormous! His only Son had to pay the price for Adam's free choice to move from temptation into sin. That one sin condemned the whole world in God's eyes.

God hates sin. Never can He accept it. Never does He compromise! The price of sin is so high that it could only be paid with a holy sacrifice. God would send His very best, His only Son, to deliver us from sin! Jesus is holy, and He was the one sacrifice God could accept.

God is extreme against sin! We can see, as a result of sin, that Adam and Eve were removed from the garden, and the world outside the garden was turned over to the sin nature. Demons were given the right, if you will, to rule the underworld and to have limited access to the sinful human race. Research into the repercussions of sin that are mentioned in the Scriptures would fill another book.

If we fast-forward to the future, we see that the Lord has a final place reserved for both the holy and the sinner. The final place mentioned in the Bible for the sinner is the lake of fire. Death and Hell will be cast there in the future at the final judgment and also anyone whose name is not found in the Lamb's Book of Life.

> *"Then death and Hades were thrown into the lake of fire. The lake of fire is the second death. If anyone's name was not found written in the book of life, he was thrown into the lake of fire."* (Revelation 20:14-15)

The lake of fire is a place not only of separation from God but also an eternal place of torment. We believers should do all we can to live a holy life and to point out salvation to as many as will listen. Without salvation through the atoning blood of Jesus, the Bible clearly states that God will have to cast His creation into the lake of eternal fire! This is the serious business of God. He has to cast His creation that He loves away from Him because of the condemnation that sin brought in Eden.

God has righteous wrath for that *one sin* in the garden. Awake to the fact that God is extreme! The good news is that the *one-time* sacrifice at the cross pays the sin penalty. Now, the person who receives the free gift of Jesus will not have to face the wrath of the Lord or the lake of fire. The future for the believer in Jesus is eternal glory in a beautiful place called "heaven." There are only two final destinations for God's creation: Heaven, or the Lake of Fire. God gives you free choice to determine where you will spend eternity.

That's the future final deal. Meanwhile, look at the other things that came after the Eden experience. The sin of Adam caused God's creation to be turned over to the sin nature. Adam's son, Cain, killed his brother, Abel. The sin nature rears its ugly head. That sin nature is against God and needs to be crucified. The ONLY acceptable sacrifice, however, had to be the Lamb of God, Jesus. The Old Testament is written to show us how creation acted before Jesus crucified sin. Take a look. It's not pretty!

> *"... for all have sinned and fall short of the glory of God ..."* (Romans 3:23 NKJV)

# CHAPTER 9

# Direct Presence Disobedience

Direct presence disobedience is recorded twice in the Bible—once in heaven and once in the garden. When Lucifer sinned, God had him hurled out of heaven (Revelation 12:7-9). The Lord is holy and is 180 degrees away from sin. God can never sin, and to be with Him, you must be holy.

That first disobedience caused the holy Lord to cast the first sinner, Lucifer, and his angels out of heaven instantly. Notice that God had zero tolerance for the direct presence disobedience of Lucifer and his angels. Their future was determined right then. Never again was that event repeated. God had to make His move right then and there. Jesus talks about a place prepared for the devil and his angels, a place called "hell."

> *"Then He will also say to those on the left hand, 'Depart from Me, you cursed, into the everlasting fire prepared for the devil and his angels ...' "* (Matthew 25:41 NKJV)

Not only did God have to cast the devil and a third of the angels out of heaven, but He also prepared a destination for them called hell. Their future final place of torment is called the lake of fire. God, you will notice, never kills because He is not a murderer and cannot murder. Because He is holy, God has to place His creation somewhere for eternity. There is free choice in heaven, yes, but one act of direct presence disobedience caused Lucifer to become Satan, and the future was sealed for him, his angels, and others who follow his lead.

Man was the next free choice creation. God created the earth and mankind in Genesis. We read about the earthly free choice. The Eden experience was a one-time event, and it was also in the direct presence of God. In Genesis, we read that the Lord was walking in the garden with His creation. The Lord is holy and had zero tolerance for the sin of Adam. Not only were Adam and Eve ejected from the garden, but the Lord had to turn the whole world over to a sin nature that was 180 degrees from His own nature.

> *"Therefore, just as through one man sin entered the world, and death through sin, and thus death spread to all men, because all sinned."* (Romans 5:12 NKJV)

## You Need To Know ...

### You Are Responsible and Held Accountable To God.

> *"For we must all appear before the judgment seat of Christ, that each one may receive what is due him for the things done while in the body, whether good or bad."* (2 Corinthians 5:10)
>
> **TOTAL VICTORY PERSPECTIVE:** ***Learn it, live it, share it!***™

# CHAPTER 10

## Take A New Look At The Old Testament

All of the Old Testament events, such as wars, immorality, lies, theft, and so on, happened because of the Eden failure. Takc notice of all the people who continually disobeyed God in the Old Testament writings. The reason they kept doing evil is because they were in the SIN NATURE. In order for men to be free, Jesus had to crucify sin. The Old Testament states that a Savior was on His way, but man amply demonstrated through thousands of years what life was like outside of God's will. Every once in a while you will notice someone doing something right in the Old Testament histories, but it was rare and usually inspired by God. After the cross, you notice that it is not the same. Jesus crucified the old nature and now gives the Holy Spirit to anyone who calls upon His name.

What about future events—the rapture, tribulation, etc.? Look into the Book of Revelation. None of this would be coming if Adam had not sinned. What about the seven bowls of wrath, the seven trumpets, the antichrist, judgment, and the lake of fire? Wow! Meditate on the Holy Lord and how extreme He has to be against sin!

So, why would it be okay for you to sin against Him today? God did not approve of the sin behavior in the Old Testament. All of the people were under condemnation from Adam's sin in the garden. They continually compounded the sin with their own versions of disobedience. Don't take this wrong, but these imperfect people were all God had to work with to tell the story and to bring about salvation. They did not yet have the promised

Messiah Who would come and crucify the sin of the world. The Old Testament people were doing what their sin natures compelled them to do: commit evil, over and over again. "Since we have now been justified by his blood, how much more shall we be saved from God's wrath through him!" (Romans 5:9).

When God sent His Son Jesus, He sent Him one time—ONE TIME—to take away the sin of the world.

> *"The next day John saw Jesus coming toward him and said, 'Look, the Lamb of God, who takes away the sin of the world!' "* (John 1:29)
>
> *"You, however, are controlled not by the sinful nature but by the Spirit, if the Spirit of God lives in you. And if anyone does not have the Spirit of Christ, he does not belong to Christ."* (Romans 8:9)
>
> *"Those who belong to Christ Jesus have crucified the sinful nature with its passions and desires."* (Galatians 5:24)
>
> *"But the fruit of the Spirit is love, joy, peace, longsuffering, kindness, goodness, faithfulness, gentleness, self-control. Against such there is no law."* (Galatians 5:22-23 NKJV)

If the thoughts in your mind are not those of the above Scriptures, IT'S A DEVIL, IT'S A DEVIL, IT'S A DEVIL!

# You Need To Know ...

## God Sent His Son Because He Loves You.

*"For God so loved the world that he gave his one and only Son, that whoever believes in him shall not perish but have eternal life."* (John 3:16)

**TOTAL VICTORY PERSPECTIVE:** ***Learn it, live it, share it!***™

# CHAPTER 11

# Can A Devil Read Your Mind?

I was talking to a pastor some time ago, and I asked him to consider the sin nature that has passed through Christ's work on the cross. Since the sin nature is crucified with Christ when you are a born again believer, the only place a temptation can come from is a devil. I call it DIA—Devil In Area. A devil is in the area passing out tempting and deceiving thoughts.

Right away, the pastor asked, "What about James talking about temptations from evil inside?" referring to James 1:14.

The pastor shared with me that sometimes while he is working on a sermon, evil thoughts come to him. He considers those thoughts to have come from the "old nature" inside of him because devils cannot read our minds.

According to the Word, he is right that devils cannot read our minds.

> *"For who among men knows the thoughts of a man except the man's spirit within him?"* (1 Corinthians 2:11)

Devils can certainly deceive the mind, however, and influence our thoughts.

> *"The Spirit clearly says that in later times some will abandon the faith and follow deceiving spirits and things taught by demons."* (1 Timothy 4:1)

There are two possible answers to the James 1:14 passage that I would like to suggest. First, what if James is talking about the lost? He starts by addressing the 12 tribes who were Jews. There were believers there also, but when James refers to temptation from evil inside a person, I believe he is referring to the unsaved. If we have accepted Christ's gift of Life, why not consider ourselves dead to sin and tempted by an outside source, a devil?

Second, what if James was referring to the human mind that has not been renewed or has not yet learned the truth of God's Word and how to recognize a DIA? We are sanctified and cleansed (from old thought patterns) with the washing of water by the Word (Ephesians 5:26). Then "... we take captive every thought to make it obedient to Christ" (2 Corinthians 10:3-5).

> *"Finally, brethren, whatever things are true, whatever things are noble, whatever things are just, whatever things are pure, whatever things are lovely, whatever things are of good report, if there is any virtue and if there is anything praiseworthy—meditate on these things."*
> (Philippians 4:8 NKJV)

The bottom line is that we are not to act on thoughts that would be displeasing to our Lord. As someone has correctly stated, "we can't stop a bird from flying over our heads, but we certainly can stop it from building a nest in our hair." So, we cannot stop thoughts from flying through our minds, but we can keep them from staying.

The mind is where I believe God allows all the supernatural communication to take place. Consider, if you will, that God sometimes allows devils to inject evil thoughts for you to pass a test, using the Scripture to do battle. Ephesians 6:10-18 says, "We wrestle not against flesh and blood ..." The Lord wants us to use His word to fight against sin and to get out of every temptation.

> *Therefore, if anyone is in Christ, he is a new creation; the old has gone, the new has come!* (2 Corinthians 5:17)

> *Those who belong to Christ Jesus have crucified the sinful nature with its passions and desires.* (Galatians 5:24)

> *For we know that our old self was crucified with him so that the body of sin might be done away with, that we should no longer be slaves to sin—because anyone who has died has been freed from sin.* (Romans 6:6-7)

# CHAPTER 12

# Devil In Area (DIA) Is A Normal Way of Life

So you're having thoughts of evil, even though you are a Christian? Yes, it is normal, and I call it a DIA (Devil In Area). God allows a DIA in your life for you to be tested, and tested only. You will be tempted by an unseen fallen angel; that's the way it works. Rejoice at the good news: God offers a way of escape, every time!

When you are tempted, there is a DIA. It is a fallen angel talking trash, but that's all it can do. If the thoughts coming to your mind are not the first three fruits of the fruit of the Spirit (Galatians 5:22-23), God is allowing a DIA for you to deal with. God wants you to pass every test that He allows to come your way. Recognize the DIA, and make the right decision with that temptation. (Later on we will explore a look at a fictional episode, behind the scenes. What if you could see into the unholy angels' realm?)

Wait! Let me clarify. Not for one minute do I say that a devil *made* you do anything. No, a devil can only tempt you, *tempt*, not compel. If they could make you disobey, then there would be a power struggle (meaning, who is going to win, God or Satan?). There is no power struggle between the Lord Almighty and His created angels who disobeyed Him. You will always have the opportunity to take your free choice and not do what they are tempting you to do. When Jesus Himself was led by the Holy Spirit to the desert, the devil only tempted Him. Jesus has no sin nature in Him, so He was only tempted, tempted from an outside source, not from a sin nature within Himself.

Jesus is pure, and there is no sin in Him. Jesus said to Satan right in his presence, "It is written ..." The devil could only tempt, and he knows that the person he tempts must make the free choice that God gives and accept the temptation himself, thereby sinning. The human creation who receives Christ will always be given a line that he should not cross. The list is in Galatians 5:19-21 (a list of sin temptations devils can and *will* use.) There is nothing new. Devils know the Word of God. Moreover, the Lord *is* the Word.

Jesus told the devil, "... it is written, 'You shall worship the Lord your God, and Him only you shall serve'" (Matthew 4:10 NKJV). He called upon the power of the Holy Spirit to resist temptation. This is the same power we are to use today when a devil tempts us. The more we know of God's Word, the stronger our stance against those disobedient unclean spirits.

Awaken to doing God's plan! This is the message I want to send to all saved people throughout the world:

**Stop failing when God allows a test to come into your lives.**

You are important to God. He wants you to be tested, not to see you fail, but to learn reliance on Him. God will allow you to use His power to stop any temptation. You do not have to be tripped up when a DIA comes your way. Training in the Word will allow you to be a righteous light for the world. You can truly be an example of the Lord and give the lost world something to crave.

You will be tested, but the Lord is on your side. Show the lost people around you how the Lord gives you power to stand against all situations without fear and without blaming God.

# CHAPTER 13

# What Does The World See You Do?

Are you living a defeated Christian life in front of the world? What hope are you offering them? Why would someone want to become a Christian if they see no difference in your life from theirs? Are you acting like the world when something difficult happens in your life?

Stop that now, and live in the power that God has supplied. I don't want you to beat yourself up; if you want to obey God, you can! Wake up to the fact that if you have been saved, God allows devils to tempt you. My perspective is, *you* don't tempt yourself! I want to point the finger at the one who is doing the tempting. I want you to lift up the rock, if you will, and see that in the spirit realm, devils are real.

Jesus is the Creator of all things, and He has not saved us with His blood for us to let a devil deceive us to disobey. The price Jesus paid was and is the final price. There is nothing left out. Jesus loves us and gave His blood to release us from sin. Let's respect that sacrifice and live for Him and not be tripped up by a devil's temptation. Shine your holy light for the entire world to see.

What kind of message are we giving the lost?

> *"... but as He who called you is holy, you also be holy in all your conduct, because it is written, 'Be holy, for I am holy.'"* (1 Peter 1:15-16 NKJV)

> *"The next day John saw Jesus coming toward him and said, 'Look, the Lamb of God, who takes away the sin of the world!'"* (John 1:29)

> *"Those who belong to Christ Jesus have crucified the sinful nature with its passions and desires."* (Galatians 5:24)

> *"... for all have sinned and fall short of the glory of God ..."* (Romans 3:23 NKJV)

Romans 3:23 is a fact! That is why we had to have Jesus—Jesus was crucified once. Now anyone can receive God's free gift and have His Spirit given to him or her by simple faith in Jesus.

We have all the power to live holy lives because of what Jesus did for us at the cross.

Who wants to join the Sin/Repent Club (SRC)? Unfortunately, without actually saying it, most Christian testimonies seem like an invitation to come and join the "Sin/Repent Club" (SRC). They say, "I am a sinner. You are a sinner. I fail God often, but He forgives me when I sin." Then we say, "Come to Jesus; you need a Savior."

The Christian realm tells the lost, "No one is perfect, even after salvation. We still fail. We're only human. Thank God for His grace, I fail Him often." WHAT? WAIT! Is that the message Jesus left us after the cross, that we are to go and sin? God had Lucifer thrown out of heaven for one sin. Adam was removed from the garden for one sin. So now God sent His Son to die for sin so you can go and sin? Really? You mean to tell me that all we have to offer the world is an invitation to join the "Sin/Repent Club"?

***Please stop telling the lost that Jesus' power is not enough! This is not a "Sin/Repent Club."***

Why don't we rethink what the supernatural power actually is after we receive Christ? Who are we after we receive Jesus Who takes away the old and gives us the new?

We have the answer the world needs. Don't tell them you are a failure after you receive Jesus. That's not who we are; we are a new creation. The old is gone. We have power over all sin to stop at temptation every time!

> *"No temptation has overtaken you except such as is common to man; but God is faithful, who will not allow you to be tempted beyond what you are able, but with the temptation will also make the way of escape, that you may be able to bear it."* (1 Corinthians 10:13 NKJV)

Please, Christian, go to the lost and say something more like: "God loves you and sent His Son to crucify sin, the sin that came in when Adam disobeyed in the Garden of Eden. When Jesus died on the cross, He died one time to crucify the sin. Jesus paid a great price for the sin of the world. If you come to Jesus, He will give you a new life, and you will be able to **stop all the sin at temptation** if you want to. When you come to Jesus, you will be able to live a pure life. Yes, you will be tempted a lot of the time, but now your free choice can be used to stop temptation and not fail God."

Tell the world they never have to fail God again. Tell them they will be tempted, but they too can take His power and say no to sin every time. Come to Jesus. He is the one sacrifice God accepts for sin. Come to Jesus, and you will be His ambassador to represent Him and show the world His power against sin. Tell them, "*If*, not *when*, you sin, you are reminded quickly by the Holy Spirit to repent right then, but why fail Him when the power to stop at temptation is ever present? Tell them if they come to Jesus, they will be a new creation and the Spirit of God will come to live inside them, keeping their minds in tune with what the devils are up to. Tell them they can be made use of to draw people to God so others do not have to go to hell in the future. They can actually make a difference in thousands of lives by receiving Jesus and living in His holy power every day. Tell them, yes, it is a hard life to stay on the straight and narrow, but it is *not* impossible. God will supply the power for victory; we have *total* victory in Jesus! Go tell them! Finally, tell them that they will, at the end of this life, go to be with God in heaven and live eternally in the presence of the Creator of the universe.

> *"Now I saw heaven opened, and behold, a white horse. And He who sat on him was called Faithful and True, and in righteousness He judges and makes war. His eyes were like a flame of fire, and on His head were many crowns. He had a name written that no one knew except Himself. He was clothed with a robe dipped in blood, and His name is called The Word of God. And the armies in heaven, clothed in fine linen, white and clean, followed Him on white horses. Now out of His mouth goes a sharp sword, that with it He should strike the nations. And He Himself will rule them with a rod of iron. He Himself treads the winepress of the fierceness and wrath of Almighty God. And He has on His robe and on His thigh a name written: KING OF KINGS AND LORD OF LORDS."* (Revelation 19:11-16 NKJV)

# You Need To Know ...

## God Sent His Son To Crucify Sin, Allowing You A New Nature.

*"Those who belong to Christ Jesus have crucified the sinful nature with its passions and desires."* (Galatians 5:24)

*"In him you were also circumcised, in the putting off of the sinful nature, not with a circumcision done by the hands of men but with the circumcision done by Christ..."* (Colossians 2:11)

*"Therefore, if anyone is in Christ, he is a new creation; the old has gone, the new has come!"* (2 Corinthians 5:17)

*"For you have been born again, not of perishable seed, but of imperishable, through the living and enduring word of God."* (1 Peter 1:23)

**TOTAL VICTORY PERSPECTIVE:** ***Learn it, live it, share it!***™

# CHAPTER 14

# God's Grace Is Not A License To Disobey

The majority of believers in the Lord Jesus that I have met are into a school of thought that says, "We are not perfect, only forgiven." Most say, "We are going to mess up, and God will forgive us. We are just human, we cannot expect to be perfect until we are in heaven with the Lord. Only Jesus was perfect, and I'm not Jesus."

Wait, didn't Jesus say in Matthew 5:48, "Be perfect, therefore, as your heavenly Father is perfect"?

I am not making fun of anyone here. I used to think the same way until the Word convicted me to stop saying, "I'm just going to mess up." I now have a free will focus to be holy for God is holy. Yes, it is fact that God will forgive you if you confess and repent of your sin. It is a guarantee. God is a loving Father who wants the best for His creation. That's why He sent His Son. Notice the Bible states in 1 John that *if we sin*, we have an Advocate, Jesus Christ. It does not say, "when we sin." So many Christians are living the life of sin, repent, then sin, and repent again. This does not line up to God's holiness and the life you are supposed to live after you receive His Son as Savior.

> *"My little children, these things I write to you, so that you may not sin. And if anyone sins, we have an Advocate with the Father, Jesus Christ the righteous."* (1 John 2:1 NKJV)

There is a big difference between living your life to believe "*when* we sin" as opposed to "*if* we sin." The "*when* we sin" acceptance is a lie! We are to never sin after Jesus crucified the old and gave the new; we are able to get out of every temptation before it is sin.

> *"No temptation has overtaken you except such as is common to man; but God is faithful, who will not allow you to be tempted beyond what you are able, but with the temptation will also make the way of escape, that you may be able to bear it."* (1 Corinthians 10:13 NKJV)

The cross was a big deal, folks. God forgave us at the cross and gave us His Spirit to live by, to live supernaturally in holiness. Do we really understand what happened at the cross? Is it just a buzzword in the Christian faith to say, "I am crucified with Christ?" Because God has given His Spirit, it is His power that will keep you from falling into temptation. Not your own power, His power. So if your free choice is to obey God, why would you be failing? All of the Lord's power is backing you for holy living.

# CHAPTER 15

# Is It Really You Keeping You From Obeying God?

You have a free choice to say no to temptation, and after you receive Jesus as Savior, it is not *you* who is tempting you!

Don't look for any red suit and pitchfork here, but the Scriptures say we do have an enemy. When my daughter was little she once said, "I know how people can know when a devil is around, Daddy. It's when they go to a costume party and see someone with a red suit, toting a pitchfork. Then you can say, 'Ahhh! It's a devil. Let's get out of here.'"

It would be a lot easier if God commanded devils to visibly appear when they are tempting you. They could wear that famous red suit, tote a pitchfork, and sport a long tail with—don't forget—the little arrow pointed at the end.

> *"Those who belong to Christ Jesus have crucified the sinful nature with its passions and desires."* (Galatians 5:24)

Huh? Or shall I say, "WOW!" Christ crucified the sinful nature supernaturally. Then what's going on? Why is my mind having thoughts that are evil temptations, thoughts that I do not want, thoughts that even make me sick? Where do these unwanted thoughts come from? Do you really want to know? God's Word shows you.

> *"Therefore, if anyone is in Christ, he is a new creation; the old has gone, the new has come!"* (2 Corinthians 5:17)

SPIRITUAL REALITY CHECK! Let's refer to our Training Manual, God's Word:

> *"Be sober, be vigilant; because your adversary the devil walks about like a roaring lion, seeking whom he may devour."* (1 Peter 5:8 NKJV)

> *"So the great dragon was cast out, that serpent of old, called the Devil and Satan, who deceives the whole world; he was cast to the earth, and his angels were cast out with him."* (Revelation 12:9 NKJV)

> *"We know that we are of God, and the whole world lies under the sway of the wicked one."* (1 John 5:19 NKJV)

> *"... nor give place to the devil."* (Ephesians 4:27 NKJV)

> *"For the weapons of our warfare are not carnal but mighty in God for pulling down strongholds, casting down arguments and every high thing that exalts itself against the knowledge of God, bringing every thought into captivity to the obedience of Christ ..."* (2 Corinthians 10:4-5 NKJV)

# You Need To Know ...

## Who Do You Fight When You Receive Jesus?

*"Finally, be strong in the Lord and in his mighty power. Put on the full armor of God so that you can take your stand against the devil's schemes. For our struggle is not against flesh and blood, but against the rulers, against the authorities, against the powers of this dark world and against the spiritual forces of evil in the heavenly realms. Therefore put on the full armor of God, so that when the day of evil comes, you may be able to stand your ground, and after you have done everything, to stand. Stand firm then, with the belt of truth buckled around your waist, with the breastplate of righteousness in place, and with your feet fitted with the readiness that comes from the gospel of peace. In addition to all this, take up the shield of faith, with which you can extinguish all the flaming arrows of the evil one. Take the helmet of salvation and the sword of the Spirit, which is the word of God. And pray in the Spirit on all occasions with all kinds of prayers and requests. With this in mind, be alert and always keep on praying for all the saints."* (Ephesians 6:10-18)

**TOTAL VICTORY PERSPECTIVE:** ***Learn it, live it, share it!***™

# CHAPTER 16

## You Are Not Your Own; God Has Chosen You.

By faith in Jesus, you have been given the Spirit of God. His Spirit is perfect and powerful; don't let any devil tell you anything different! Hey, let's get a perspective on this. Before Satan was allowed to come to earth and tempt Eve to disobey, the Scripture tells us we were already known by God.

> *"For he chose us in him before the creation of the world to be holy and blameless in his sight."* (Ephesians 1:4)

God knows all things and sees through and past eternity, right? God created, and as He created, He saw everyone and their FREE CHOICE. As someone takes his or her choice to go God's way, God sees that and He supplies the power for that person to be in right standing with Him. A person is not a robot, so God always allows a free choice to go His way or not. As God saw you and your free choice to accept Him, He chose to give you His power to obey Him, before the foundation of the earth. God wants His creation to come to Him by their free choice.

Once you know who you are in the Lord, you become immovable against anything or anybody, seen or unseen. Chosen before the world was here. WOW! Isn't God great? He chose you to be pure and blameless. Why would God tell you to be something He knew you could not achieve? God is not a rude game player and certainly not a liar. In Ephesians 2:8-10, the Word tells us that God created us for good works, not failure. Sure, we can mess up, repent, mess up, and repent. It is a free choice. But why are we striving with failure instead of striving to be holy and pleasing in His sight? We need to look at what God said: "Be holy for I am holy." God never said, "Be average for I am holy," or "Go ye and be mediocre for I am holy."

MAKE YOUR DECISION NOW; TAKE YOUR STAND! I will take my free choice and be like Joshua.

> *"And if it seems evil to you to serve the LORD, choose for yourselves this day whom you will serve, whether the gods which your fathers served that were on the other side of the River, or the gods of the Amorites, in whose land you dwell. But as for me and my house, we will serve the LORD."* (Joshua 24:15 NKJV)

Yes, I say the same: "As for me and my house, we will serve the Lord." Do you have anything in your life for which you have not repented? Repent from all unrighteousness, confess to the Lord, and He will forgive you. Do not give the devil a foothold! Now go and sin no more.

In John 8:1-11, Jesus told the woman caught in adultery and brought to Him by the religious leaders, "Go and sin no more." Strive for purity in the Lord. Put on the full armor of God. Devils are all liars. Dear child of God, Jesus has crucified the sin nature that was in you. Cast down any thoughts that come to your mind that are disobedient to the Lord God Almighty.

> *"For the weapons of our warfare are not carnal but mighty in God for pulling down strongholds, casting down arguments and every high thing that exalts itself against the knowledge of God, bringing every thought into captivity to the obedience of Christ..."* (2 Corinthians 10:4-5 NKJV)

> *"If we confess our sins, He is faithful and just to forgive us our sins and to cleanse us from all unrighteousness."* (1 John 1:9 NKJV)

Notice that after the confession, there is forgiveness. Also notice that it says He will "cleanse us from *all* unrighteousness," not "go and sin and repent."

> *"And everyone who has this hope in Him purifies himself, just as He is pure."* (1 John 3:3 NKJV)

# CHAPTER 17

# Why Did Jesus Have To Come Down To Earth?

When this question is asked, believers will say, "Because we are sinners." That is a good answer!

> *"Therefore, just as through one man sin entered the world, and death through sin, and thus death spread to all men, because all sinned."* (Romans 5:12 NKJV)

But why are we still sinners? What happened to cause us to be in need of God's wonderful grace? His free gift was given from Himself to us, the sacrifice of His only begotten Son.

> *"I thank you, Lord Jesus, for obeying Your Father. You were the only one in the universe who could come and pay the price for the disobedience (sin) in the garden. Thank You for giving Your life for me. I praise You for giving me eternal life. You alone are worthy of all honor. Holy Lord, I worship You and desire to obey Your Word."*

The Word of God tells us exactly why Jesus came:

> *"He who sins is of the devil, for the devil has sinned from the beginning. For this purpose the Son of God was manifested, that He might destroy the works of the devil."* (1 John 3:8 NKJV)

*"Inasmuch then as the children have partaken of flesh and blood, He Himself likewise shared in the same, that through death He might destroy him who had the power of death, that is, the devil ..."* (Hebrews 2:14)

There it is: Jesus came to destroy the works of the devil, not for a picnic. Jesus was the only One who could do it, and He DID!

Jesus died for you!

Think about Christ's body being beaten, His holy face spat upon, and a crown of thorns pressed upon His head ... the blood dripping down His face, nails driven through the flesh of His hands and feet, and a spear thrust into His sid ... He was suspended between heaven and earth. The earth He created was receiving His precious blood. He was offered as a sacrifice for you and me for the forgiveness of sin ... Oh, the pain and the suffering that He had to endure because of one sin, one disobedient act against God. A price had to be paid by the Son of man, the holy Lamb of God. Thank You, Lord, thank You.

But Satan's devils are getting you to say this is not enough. You say, "Oh, I would never say anything like that. I love the Lord." Yes, I believe you do, and I also love Him. Now, will you believe what God said, or will you listen to a devil that has been condemned to spend eternity in the lake of fire, a fallen angel who hates you and would love to see you destroyed. Take another look at Galatians 5:24, "Those who belong to Christ Jesus have crucified the sinful nature with its passions and desires."

Imagine Jesus coming to your living room, sitting down at a seat across from you, looking into your eyes, and saying, "Be holy for I am holy." Then He gets up and leaves. Would you take Him seriously?

> "... but as He who called you is holy, you also be holy in all your conduct, because it is written, 'Be holy, for I am holy.' " (1 Peter 1:15-16 NKJV)

# You Need To Know ...

## Who You Are
## When You Receive Jesus?

*"But the fruit of the Spirit is love, joy, peace, patience, kindness, goodness, faithfulness, gentleness and self-control. Against such things there is no law."* (Galatians 5:22-23 NIV)

**TOTAL VICTORY PERSPECTIVE:** ***Learn it, live it, share it!***™

# CHAPTER 18

## Why Not This Perspective?

Crucified! Dead! What more does the Word of God need to say? Jesus has crucified the sin nature. It is not alive any longer in you when you come to Him. The old nature does not belong to us; it belongs to the world, the world of sin.

> *"Therefore, if anyone is in Christ, he is a new creation; the old has gone, the new has come!"* (2 Corinthians 5:17)

It is written, "Be holy." That is possible only because when you receive Jesus, you receive His Holy Spirit. It's strange to think about, but there is no other explanation. God is holy and tells you to BE the same. The world is born into sin. Jesus came and died to set you free from sin. Temptation is all that a devil can do after the cross.

The Bible shows that it is completely possible to "be holy" and stop every temptation before sin takes over. What a trip! The world is in sin; everyone born after the Garden of Eden is born with a sin nature. The whole world is turned over to that nature of sin, but in Christ, the old is gone! God allows temptations to come, but never wants you to fall. Temptations are to stop right there. Do not give in to them and cross over to sin.

What a wonderful God we have Who is completely holy. Even though Adam sinned, our God sent His Son to free us from sin and allows us to stay in complete holiness. It is a mind bender!

Believe me, when the Lord revealed this to me, I was completely in awe! I was truly amazed at the love of God and His holy realm. Pure unchanging God! What a tremendous honor to know Him and live by His power. The angels who sinned are used to tempt us only until they are sent to the lake of fire.

> *"In him you were also circumcised, in the putting off of the sinful nature, not with a circumcision done by the hands of men but with the circumcision done by Christ ..."* (Colossians 2:11)

Christ paid the price. It is finished. What Jesus did on the cross was a big deal, the biggest ever. Without the shedding of blood, there is no forgiveness of sin. He was the only sacrifice that God would accept. He did it! Yes, it is finished by God's grace. Thank You Lord! Do not let the devils deceive you into believing that the thoughts in your mind that are against God are yours. IT'S A DEVIL; IT'S A DEVIL; IT'S A DEVIL!

# CHAPTER 19

# Now Is The Time To Stop The Disobedience.

Okay, it's time to get excited! Here are the verses that will give you insight to an understanding that is new to us. This is what our Lord did for us at the cross.

Galatians 5:19-21 has transformed my life! As I share this Scripture with others, their lives are also being transformed by God's awesome Word. I pray the Lord will allow you to be set free from this day forward. May God break any stronghold that the enemy has on you or your family! By the power of His word and direction of the Spirit, may you receive His deliverance from all the powers of darkness! I ask all these things in Jesus' name. Amen.

> *"Now the works of the flesh are evident, which are: adultery, fornication, uncleanness, lewdness, idolatry, sorcery, hatred, contentions, jealousies, outbursts of wrath, selfish ambitions, dissensions, heresies, envy, murders, drunkenness, revelries, and the like; of which I tell you beforehand, just as I also told you in time past, that those who practice such things will not inherit the kingdom of God."* (Galatians 5:19 –21 NKJV)

Did you see it? "Those who practice such things will not inherit the kingdom." The world practices such things because the people are locked into the works of the flesh. Without receiving Jesus, there is no way out of the sin nature. You, as a believer in Christ, are not of the world any longer. Once you accepted Christ, you were crucified to the world.

*"But God forbid that I should boast except in the cross of our Lord Jesus Christ, by whom the world has been crucified to me, and I to the world."* (Galatians 6:14 NKJV)

The sin nature came into the world because of the disobedience of Adam.

*"For as by one man's disobedience many were made sinners, so also by one Man's obedience many will be made righteous."* (Romans 5:19 NKJV)

By the obedience of the Son of God, Jesus Christ, the sin nature was crucified.

*"And those who are Christ's have crucified the flesh with its passions and desires."* (Galatians 5:24 NKJV)

The sin nature is a strange thing. It is 180 degrees opposite from God. It is the nature that is opposed to God. The world is controlled by the sin nature and cannot get rid of it. The world is condemned unless Christ is the personal Savior He claims to be. If you have received the Lord as your personal Savior, do not let a devil tell you that you are condemned. It is a lie.

*"Therefore, there is now no condemnation for those who are in Christ Jesus..."* (Romans 8:1 NIV)

*"Those controlled by the sinful nature cannot please God. You, however, are controlled not by the sinful nature but by the Spirit, if the Spirit of God lives in you. And if anyone does not have the Spirit of Christ, he does not belong to Christ."* (Romans 8:8-9 NIV)

The qualification for you to NOT be controlled by the sinful nature is that you must have the Holy Spirit living inside you. The following verse shows that you are given the Spirit once you trusted Jesus as your Savior.

*"In Him you also trusted, after you heard the word of truth, the gospel of your salvation; in whom also, having believed, you were sealed with the Holy Spirit of promise, who is the guarantee of our inheritance until the redemption of the purchased possession, to the praise of His glory."* (Ephesians 1:13-14 NKJV)

God is just. If anyone will call upon the name of Jesus, they can be delivered from the power of darkness.

The characteristics of the sin nature are listed in the next chapter. As a Christian, I believe this list has been crucified. This is the list that Satan and his devils will use against you. Devils will inject a thought into your mind, then deceive you into thinking and finally believing that it is your own personal thought. This can happen in seconds. You are dealing with devils, and they are 100% liars.

# CHAPTER 20

# Which Thoughts Do The Devils Have You Thinking Are Yours?

- ADULTERY—voluntary sexual activity between a married man and a woman not his wife or between a married woman and a man not her husband.
- FORNICATION—voluntary sexual activity generally forbidden by law between an unmarried woman and a man.
- UNCLEANNESS—morally impure, unchaste, obscene or vile behavior.
- LICENTIOUSNESS—morally unrestrained sexual activity.
- IDOLATRY—worship of idols, excessive devotion to or reverence for some person or thing.
- SORCERY—witchcraft, magic.
- HATRED—strong dislike or ill will.
- CONTENTIONS—strife, struggle, controversy, disputes, quarreling.
- JEALOUSIES—resentfully suspicious of a rival or a rival's influence; a husband jealous of other men.
- OUTBURSTS OF WRATH—sudden release of anger, yelling, screaming.

◎ SELFISH AMBITION—too much concern with one's own welfare or interests and having little or no concern for others; self-centered.

◎ DISSENSIONS—violent quarreling or wrangling; to argue.

◎ HERESIES—a religious belief specifically denounced by the church; opposed to official or established views or doctrines.

◎ ENVY—a feeling of discontent and ill will because of another's advantages, possessions, etc.

◎ MURDERS—killing of God's creation; killing of oneself.

◎ DRUNKENNESS—overcome by alcoholic liquor to a point of losing control.

◎ REVELRIES—noisy merrymaking, boisterous festivity; crude, unmannerly, violent.

# PART 2

## KNOW YOUR ENEMY

# CHAPTER 21

## Who Is This Devil Anyway?

God created a beautiful angel that went against Him.

> *"You were the seal of perfection, full of wisdom and perfect in beauty. You were in Eden, the garden of God; every precious stone was your covering: the sardius, topaz, and diamond, beryl, onyx, and jasper, sapphire, turquoise, and emerald with gold. The workmanship of your timbrels and pipes was prepared for you on the day you were created. You were the anointed cherub who covers; I established you; you were on the holy mountain of God; you walked back and forth in the midst of fiery stones. You were perfect in your ways from the day you were created, till iniquity was found in you. By the abundance of your trading you became filled with violence within, and you sinned; therefore I cast you as a profane thing out of the mountain of God; and I destroyed you, O covering cherub, from the midst of the fiery stones. Your heart was lifted up because of your beauty; you corrupted your wisdom for the sake of your splendor; I cast you to the ground, I laid you before kings, that they might gaze at you. You defiled your sanctuaries by the multitude of your iniquities, by the iniquity of your trading; therefore I brought fire from your midst; it devoured you, and I turned you to ashes upon the earth in the sight of all who saw you. All who knew you among the peoples are astonished at you; you have become a horror, and shall be no more forever."* (Ezekiel 28:12b-19 NKJV)

Next we see that Lucifer says that he is going to be like God. There sure are a lot of religions out there that say they are gods or will someday be a god. This is what got ol' Lucifer in trouble. God still hates disobedience. No one is God except God. Whether anyone in the world or the universe likes it or not,

He is the Lord God Almighty. God loves the world and sent His Son to protect creation from Satan. God wants everyone to be saved. You have a free choice to receive His paid-for gift. The Lord wants to give us love, joy, and peace. Satan has tricked the world into staying away from God. Satan is the father of lies. It is so wonderful that we have a God who is Almighty and perfect. No sin can ever enter heaven; all disobedience will be corrected. No one gets away with anything, not the angels, not the humans, nobody. Rejection of God's holiness is not tolerated. Talk about zero tolerance, God is the originator of it. He hates sin. Take a look:

> *"How you are fallen from heaven, O Lucifer, son of the morning! How you are cut down to the ground, you who weakened the nations! For you have said in your heart: 'I will ascend into heaven, I will exalt my throne above the stars of God; I will also sit on the mount of the congregation on the farthest sides of the north; I will ascend above the heights of the clouds, I will be like the Most High.' Yet you shall be brought down to Sheol, to the lowest depths of the Pit. Those who see you will gaze at you, and consider you, saying: 'Is this the man who made the earth tremble, who shook kingdoms, who made the world as a wilderness and destroyed its cities, who did not open the house of his prisoners?'"* (Isaiah 14:12-17 NKJV)

What happened in heaven with Lucifer? Lucifer, a being created by God Himself, went against the Lord with his plan to overthrow the Lord's government in his own evil way. Lucifer took his free choice in heaven, living in the presence of God Almighty, and chose to disobey. Man, what an arrogant being this Lucifer was! Think about it: He was created by God, lived in the presence of God, and he still chose to disobey. In your human strength, there is no way you can fight this guy. He is evil like no other and will stop at nothing to destroy God's creation. Learn how to fight him in the Spirit. You can't go wrong! God is backing you with His holy power. Disobedience to God brought the following consequences.

> *"And there was war in heaven. Michael and his angels fought against the dragon, and the dragon and his angels fought back. But he was not strong enough, and they lost their place in heaven. The great dragon was hurled down – that ancient serpent called the devil, or Satan, who leads the whole world astray. He was hurled to the earth, and his angels with him."*
> (Revelation 12:7-9)

So they lost their place in heaven and went to the earth to rest? NO!

> *"And the dragon was enraged with the woman, and he went to make war with the rest of her offspring, who keep the commandments of God and have the testimony of Jesus Christ."* (Revelation 12:17 NKJV)

How many angels went with the dragon?

> *"His tail drew a third of the stars of heaven and threw them to the earth."* (Revelation 12:4a NKJV)

One third...of what quantity? The Word never specifically states the number of angels God created, or does it?

> *"Then I looked, and I heard the voice of many angels around the throne, the living creatures, and the elders; and the number of them was ten thousand times ten thousand, and thousands of thousands..."*
> (Revelation 5:11 NKJV)

This passage is talking about angels around the throne at one particular time. Do you wonder how many angels are in God's universe? The following verse gives us more insight.

> *"But you have come to Mount Zion and to the city of the living God, the heavenly Jerusalem, to an innumerable company of angels ..."*
> (Hebrews 12:22 NKJV)

I was asking the Lord about the number. We humans look at the ratio like this: We know two-thirds are good angels and one-third are bad devils, and we have a big world. What about this perspective: two-thirds angels and one-third devils, and a very small world in a very large universe? This would mean there are plenty of devils to go around. Oh, boy, devils everywhere, maybe trillions, not omnipresent (present everywhere at the same time) for sure, but a boatload for the war against God's creation. Don't be afraid. Jesus is the final Word. Jesus gives us power over the enemy every time!

> *"But the Lord is faithful, who will establish you and guard you from the evil one."* (2 Thessalonians 3:3 NKJV)

There are a lot of angels out there, alive and well. One third are fallen, looking for someone to destroy. They can only tempt a believer in Jesus. Because the sin nature is crucified, the only way a believer can disobey God is to listen to a direct devil attack. This means that devils are right there with you even though you can't see them—not possessing a believer, no way—because you have been given the Spirit of God. There are not two natures living in you. God gave you the Holy Spirit, which is pure. When you receive Christ, you are given the Holy Spirit. The devils' deception is to get you believing that the thoughts coming to your mind to disobey God are from your own sin nature. I believe the truth is that Jesus totally delivers all who call on His name.

## You Need To Know ...

## Who You Are Not When You Receive Jesus?

*"The acts of the sinful nature are obvious: sexual immorality, impurity and debauchery; idolatry and witchcraft; hatred, discord, jealousy, fits of rage, selfish ambition, dissensions, factions and envy; drunkenness, orgies, and the like. I warn you, as I did before, that those who live like this will not inherit the kingdom of God."* (Galatians 5:19-21)

**TOTAL VICTORY PERSPECTIVE:** ***Learn it, live it, share it!***™

# CHAPTER 22

# The Garden of Eden Was Perfect Until...

The Lord spoke to me about the garden, "Did you notice that Satan could not grab Eve's arm and force her to take the fruit, nor could the devil slap the fruit into her face and make her eat it. No, she was only tempted —there was no sin in her at the time—she was tempted from an outside source, the devil. Eve had to do the act herself. She exercised her free choice."

So it is today. God's people can only be tempted. They will have to take the temptation to the next level themselves and choose to sin. They will have to exercise their free choice and disobey because a devil cannot force them to go against what the Lord wants, ever!

Come on, folks. The devils are not stupid in knowing that God gives free choice. But if, in your free choice, you choose to disobey, then you are the one who is in trouble with God, not a demon. They are already in trouble with God. The devils disobeyed in heaven and got thrown out. Now they tempt you, but it is you and your free choice that will have to do the disobedience. They cannot do it for you. God never wants you to take your free choice and sin. Never!

So, it looks like the first disobedience happened in heaven when Lucifer took his free choice and decided to go against God. Lucifer's move: Choosing to disobey. God's move: You're out of heaven! Jesus said in Matthew 10:18 that he saw Satan fall like lightning from heaven. In Revelation 12:7-9, the dragon and his angels were cast down to earth.

That brings us to the next free choice, which was in the Garden of Eden. This scene stars God, features Adam and Eve, and introduces the devil. God gave Adam plenty of warning in Genesis 2:16-17 not to eat of the tree of the knowledge of good and evil. Eve was tempted by the devil in verse 5, where the devil told her she would be like God, knowing good and evil. Humankind was still okay right then; it was only a temptation.

What a deal! Adam and Eve, this was your free choice opportunity to obey God or not. Your decision was … to disobey. Wrong decision!

The devil knew that if he could get Adam and Eve to disobey, then God would have to condemn them. God is a Holy God, and no disobedience goes unpunished.

Adam's disobedience cursed the entire world with the sin nature. Before Adam went against God, there was no sin on earth. Adam's disobedience brought in condemnation for all mankind. That one little act of disobedience was a big deal. One sin against God caused the fall of man, and sin entered the world. That's the bad news.

The good news is that God now asks us individually the same question, "Do you choose to obey?" Yes, or no?

God Himself sent His Son to pay the penalty for sin, to crucify the sin nature, and to redeem man to Himself when they go to Him in faith through Christ. In Christ, we are free from the sin and free not to sin (though Christians are often tempted by a DIA).

When we return to God through Jesus Christ, we have right standing with God once again as it was in the Garden of Eden before the disobedience. What a sacrifice God made by sending His Son to straighten out all that was corrupted in the Garden.

# CHAPTER 23

## How Devils See Things ...

Devils hate you because you are chosen by God to inherit the kingdom out of which they were thrown. Don't think for a moment that you don't have an enemy.

Ephesians 6 tells us about a tuned-up, highly skilled and structured, militant force of devils. They have several different ranks and levels and a mission to destroy. Devils are dedicated to their mission, but you, as a powerful, Spirit-controlled Christian, do what God says to do. The devils are serious, deadly serious, in their business to steal, kill, and destroy. How serious are you?

Do not look for a red suit, horns, or pitchfork. You will be tremendously mistaken if you do. We, as believers, need to be serious about our position to stand against the powers of darkness. Let us not be moved by the devils' tricks. They will attack, but we can recognize their ploy and be ready with the defense, which is found in the Word of God. Remember that the Word of God is called a Sword.

> *"He has delivered us from the power of darkness and conveyed us into the kingdom of the Son of His love ..."* (Colossians 1:13 NKJV)

He *has* delivered us, not "He is *going to* help us *some day*."

> *"Similarly, if anyone competes as an athlete, he does not receive the victor's crown unless he competes according to the rules."* (2 Timothy 2:5)

DON'T GIVE IN TO TEMPTATION! Sin brings in strongholds, and unrepentant sin gives devils *spiritual rights* to your realm. If you are deceived to sin, then when will you repent? It can take years to deal with some strongholds, even a lifetime, all the way to the grave. Don't allow that to happen!

Devils deceive believers into breaking the rules, but even devils have to operate within God's rule. Check out the book of Job in the Old Testament. Get some perspective on devils. Jesus is King of kings. Our holy Lord establishes the rules. Devils cannot create a gnat.

The Lord uses His creation to fulfill His purposes. Even those angels who disobeyed and are condemned to the Lake of Fire have to abide by God's rules. The demon can only tempt. That is in the rules God made. But the devils are allowed by the Lord to be on your turf. The Lord watches all events; He is the Most High. Thank you, Jesus! Please, Lord, let the reader receive the truth of Your Word!

God created all things, even the angels that fell. God did not want them to sin against Him; He gave them free choice to obey or not to obey just like he has given us.

Jesus is not caught off guard by devils' tricks. Don't worry, the Lord has everything under control. We are constantly in training, some days more than others, and some days we feel crushed. We may *feel* crushed, but the truth is we are *more than conquerors* through the power of Jesus Christ!

> *"Yet in all these things we are more than conquerors through Him who loved us."* (Romans 8:37 NKJV)

Whenever your feelings don't line up to the Word, ask the Lord to show you how not to be anxious for anything, to trust His power in all situations. You see, the devils' job is to deceive the believer into believing that what God said about them in His Holy Word is not true. How do they do it? Simple, they work in the invisible realm of the mind.

Now, why is it that we start backing up in the Christian realm when talking about devils that we do not see? We also have never seen Jesus, yet we know that we *know* He is here! Devils inject thoughts that would be disobedient to God, then deceive you into receiving the thoughts as if they were your own. It is weird to talk about an unseen spiritual world. The devils like that because you start blaming yourself for the disobedient thought that came to your mind.

Why would you be telling yourself to disobey the Lord that you love? It is not your thought; it is a devil!

The unseen battle is raging, and if you don't know how to fight, you most likely are not going to win. The war is already won; the Lord has already paid the price. The Lord did not need us to help Him with the war, and the devils are condemned to the lake of fire. Jesus has no power struggle with Satan. We are allowed in these battles for several reasons:

1. The Lord wants us to be conformed to the image of the Son.

   *"For whom He foreknew, He also predestined to be conformed to the image of His Son, that He might be the firstborn among many brethren."* (Romans 8:29 NKJV)

2. The Lord wants to stack up more treasure for you in heaven.

   *"Blessed be the God and Father of our Lord Jesus Christ, who according to His abundant mercy has begotten us again to a living hope through the resurrection of Jesus Christ from the dead, to an inheritance incorruptible and undefiled and that does not fade away, reserved in heaven for you ..."* (1 Peter 1:3-4 NKJV)

3. God wants you to be able to go through the battles to help someone else.

   *"Praise be to the God and Father of our Lord Jesus Christ, the Father of compassion and the God of all comfort, who comforts us in all our troubles, so that we can comfort those in any trouble with the comfort we ourselves have received from God."* (2 Corinthians 1:3-4)

Let's go back to the list from Galatians 5:19-21 showing the crucified sin nature. The devils will use whatever they can off that list to get you off track, and once off track, they will keep you in the deception of thinking this sin is okay and that these thoughts are your own. The devils will tell you, "You can't help yourself. Look, you're doing the acts. It's you. You are just a weak Christian who can't really serve God, but that's okay. God will forgive you."

What the devil is not telling you is that you are opening a dangerous door and allowing them access, not only to *your* life, but to the family around you.

Devils do not play fair! They will not tell you that you are disconnecting the power of the Lord, distancing your intimacy with Jesus. Because you can't see devils, it is easy for them to deceive you into disobedience to God.

When a devil has you convinced to do what is shameful before the Lord and you actually go and do it, it may take years to reap the harvest that was sown and to repent from this sin.

The devils will not only waste your time every time, look at what they are stealing, killing, and destroying. Don't give in to their lies.

# CHAPTER 24

## Devils Twist Truth In Your Mind...

Devils inject a thought, then watch to see how you respond. If you do not respond to a temptation by pondering whether to make it become sin, then they leave until a more opportune time.

We should use every temptation as an opportunity to rejoice in the Lord and to pray for someone. (The Lord is right there, watching and wanting you to stand.)

Devils have been watching human activity for centuries, and they know how to make you flinch. Once you show a reaction that you are pondering the temptation to disobey God, they drive in more and more thoughts and amplify them until you are actually deceived into committing the act that leads to sin.

Devils know that if they can convince you to sin, then you will be in wrong standing with God, and His correction will be upon you. The thing to remember is that when a devil has a stronghold on you, it may take you years and years to repent and get right with the Lord. Whenever you are in the middle of a sinful life, it is not impossible but mighty hard for you to repent because devils have basically deceived you into *not* repenting. The hope is, prayerfully, that others are standing in the gap for you and praying for devils to get their filthy hands off of you.

Devils can tell you God is ashamed of you and that you can't expect Him to want to help you after what you did. Or devils will say that it's no big deal, every Christian messes up. They will tell you that you are saved, and you don't need to be trying to live some pure life because it's impossible. Devils will say, "Look around; feel the moment! Yes, do whatever makes you feel good, and God will understand. He won't hold it against you when you sin." The devil will mock you with: "All have sinned and fall short of the glory of God," using God's own words deceptively. Devils will waste your time. Sometimes they even tell you to kill yourself: "You're no good; you are a loser."

The devils cannot kill you, so they work on your mind, trying to convince you to do the job yourself. What a cheap shot to have you stand before God Who loves you and threaten Him, saying, "God, I am going to destroy what You have created." (Even though someone would not actually WANT to say this to God, this is what the devil tricks you into saying by your actions.) Devils will use this method of self-murder as often as possible. It is an act that inflicts a lot of damage to those family members and friends left with the death. If a devil can remove a believer, that makes his job easier—one more that he doesn't have to fool with. Remember their mission: steal, kill, destroy.

Look at the garden: Satan did not tell Eve what would happen if she disobeyed God, did he? Devils love to use the Word against you whenever they can. Misquoting God's Word makes things sound more righteous.

> *"Be diligent to present yourself approved to God, a worker who does not need to be ashamed, rightly dividing the word of truth."* (2 Timothy 2:15 NKJV)

Devils still will not tell a believer who sins all that will be brought down upon him and how many years will be wasted.

Beautiful little devils, aren't they? No! Jesus calls them unclean spirits. Do not be surprised at what the devils come up with. The list is printed for us in Galatians 5:19-21. This is what devils can use on you. There is nothing new!

Thank God for His Word of truth! If the thought coming to your mind is not love, joy, or peace, it's a DIA (Devil In Area). Do not sin, but recognize and stop at temptation. You can use every temptation from a DIA to rejoice in the Lord and pray for someone. It works every time.

Try this: A thought comes in from a DIA (Devil In Area) to sin. If it is not love, joy, or peace coming to your mind, PUSH the pause button, rejoice in the Lord, and pray for someone! You cannot go wrong rejoicing in the Lord and praying for someone.

# You Need To Know …

## How To Stop At Temptation Before Sin

*"No temptation has seized you except what is common to man. And God is faithful; he will not let you be tempted beyond what you can bear. But when you are tempted, he will also provide a way out so that you can stand up under it."* (1 Corinthians 10:13)

*"For though we live in the world, we do not wage war as the world does. The weapons we fight with are not the weapons of the world. On the contrary, they have divine power to demolish strongholds. We demolish arguments and every pretension that sets itself up against the knowledge of God, and we take captive every thought to make it obedient to Christ."* (2 Corinthians 10:3-5)

**TOTAL VICTORY PERSPECTIVE:** ***Learn it, live it, share it!***™

# CHAPTER 25

## The Best Defense Against Satan And His Buds

The best defense against Satan is the Sword of the Spirit, the Word of God, in its entirety and with accuracy. Do not just go to church on one day and live in compromise the other six days. As a believer in the Lord, you will not be doing yourself any favor in this life or the life eternal if you allow compromise. Take your stand against the powers of darkness by making up your mind right now and saying, "I choose to obey the Lord, period, end of statement."

The pastor feeds you while you are at church. The Word is going forth. If not, pray that the Lord, by His Spirit, will convict the pastor to preach truth. If the Word is not being taught, you may have to find a church where God's Word is being preached. I always say to stay and pray as long as the pastor is standing on the Word. You can always pray and watch God move in the music or drama or whatever else you may think needs to be different at the church you attend.

Keep in mind: *It's not about you; it's about Jesus*! The key here is to see what God wants to do with all situations. If you are having thoughts from devils about being hateful toward the pastor or anyone at your church, it is a trigger for you to use. The proper response is to pray for the pastor and others as you are tempted to hate them. Hate is crucified. You are being tempted to hate, maybe, but stop it at temptation and recognize that God wants you to rejoice and pray for someone.

NEWS ALERT: God allows temptation right there at your church, not for you to fail but to use victory to rejoice in Him and pray for someone. Use every temptation as an opportunity to rejoice in the Lord and pray for the person you are being tempted against. If every Christian would recognize temptation and use it as a trigger to cause them to rejoice and pray for someone, the Christian realm would be shaken overnight. The shaking would be the rejoicing that would be lifted up to heaven and the temptations would be stopped at temptation instead of sin.

*Sin* is temptation *acted* upon! As you are tempted, stop it there, rejoice in the Lord and ask, "Is this thought love, joy, or peace?" Again, if the thought is not the first three characteristics listed in Galatians 5:22-23 (the fruit of the Spirit), then push the pause button. Stop that devil that is tempting you, use the situation to rejoice in the Lord, and pray for the person you were tempted to sin against. I see contention, envy, and selfish ambition tests failing at most churches.

God does not allow temptation so you will fail, but most Christians do not stop at temptation. They commit the sin. *If you are sinning, you are failing the test!* You are supposed to use God's power to resist the temptation and recognize from Ephesians 6 who we fight against. Recognize the attack and block it at temptation *every* time. It is God's power for you. Use it!

The bottom line is that devils cannot stand against a tuned-up believer, *ever*! God will always deliver you from any and all situations that would allow you to fall into disobedience! Guaranteed!

> *"No temptation has overtaken you except such as is common to man; but God is faithful, who will not allow you to be tempted beyond what you are able, but with the temptation will also make the way of escape, that you may be able to bear it."* (1 Corinthians 10:13 NKJV)

There is no reason to hold back. Now is the time to get things right. Knowing and using God's Word will always block a satanic attack, *always*! If there is compromise in your life, give it up right now. Repent from the past, receive God's forgiveness, and *go and sin no more*!

Maybe you thought you were just a little evil, not as bad as others. The Bible says in 1 John 3:8 that the ones who sin are of the devil. We sure don't want to be associated with him!

Maybe you need to call someone who has done you wrong and forgive him or her. Maybe you did someone wrong, and you need to tell them you are sorry. Don't let some devil keep you from all that God wants for you. Hatred and unforgiveness are not yours; they have been crucified!

It may be that you think it is okay to watch compromising movies. Those images flash back of immorality, filthy language, and horrible violence, and they haunt your mind. Your heart is heavy because you know it is not right, and you just want to forget those scenes. Forgiveness is waiting for you. Ask the Lord to forgive you for taking His Holy Spirit to see things of which you know He does not approve. He will cleanse your mind and give you restoration and peace. The fruit of the Spirit is love, joy, peace ... this is what Christ wants for you.

Maybe you have a collection of books or movies or magazines that you thought were okay to keep around, but, lately, the Spirit of the Lord has been convicting you. Your heart is heavy, and you know you need to throw them in the trash. Maybe your mind is being told (DIA) not to throw something away because it cost a lot of money. God will honor you if you serve Him; throw it in the trash if it's not what you would want to show Jesus, your Savior. Do not compromise. Don't even sell any videos, music, etc., to someone else. Throw it out like you would devils. They want us to hold on to unclean things, so the devils can have a stronghold to use. Maybe it's not apparent now. Maybe devils are holding the trump card for a greater setup for destruction for you or someone you love in the near future. Don't take a chance with devils. They will kick your backside fast if they have an entrance. Believe me, you don't know what you're dealing with when they have their foot in your door.

If you don't want to give up something that is evil, think about this: It is a devil telling you to hold on to evil. By the mercy of the Lord I say, dear friend, don't play in the devils' back yard. They are extremely skillful at deception. Don't leave any doors of compromise open in your life, period. So what if you paid a few dollars for something? God gives you the breath of life, so He can give you your money back sevenfold if it is His will. You were purchased with the blood of Jesus. Does Jesus want you to be looking at and listening to the acts of the nature He crucified?

What kind of music are you allowing into your mind? Does it lift up the name of Jesus? I'm not saying that all secular music is bad; just ask the Lord!

There are plenty of Christian bands out there. Every beat, from gospel, country, rock, rap, or whatever, can lift your thoughts to Jesus. He owns us; we should focus our lives on service to Him. Nothing else is worth Jesus. Nothing in the whole world matters except the Lord. Check Galatians 5:19-21 again, and if there is anything in your life that matches the list, drop it and repent now. Don't let a devil tell you to hold on to what has been crucified.

Now that you know, it is your free choice to serve the Lord or not. Don't get down on yourself when a thought to disobey comes to your mind or your eyes. You do not have to receive that thought, and you can always look away if a temptation is in your path. God supplies His Spirit so that you can serve Him with purity.

It is a strange, mind-bending thing to really catch hold of the fact that a devil is injecting thoughts into your mind, and it's not you. Why would you want to put thoughts into your own mind to sin against God, when you said you want to obey God? It doesn't make any sense when you finally realize what the Word says about the crucified sin nature in Galatians 5:24.

Why does your mind have temptations when you are to be holy? The thoughts are coming from an evil entity outside you. But why does God allow these devils to tempt you?

# CHAPTER 26

# Why Does God Allow Christians To Be Attacked?

Let's clarify one thing now so there are no misunderstandings: The only devil attack that you, as a believer, want in your life is a God-allowed devil attack, not an attack that is being brought on because you have been deceived to sin against God.

If you are in the middle of some sin, like leaving your spouse at home once a week so you can go get drunk and party with friends, don't expect God to bless your life. In fact, because you are property of Jesus Who said, "Be holy," it is a devil who is telling you to go do these acts. If you want to think it is you and you choose to keep sinning, you are being controlled by devils, and you are subject to God's correction.

Devils won't let you stop with partying. They will, for example, put it in your mind to indulge in sexual immorality. You see, when you are under attack by a devil and you are personally failing because you keep on going from temptation to sinning, it gets all twisted and the sins just keep stacking up more and more. You must repent, truly repent, to have the sin "ball and chain" removed and to break the cycle of sin!

I hope this is clear to you now. The only attack you want from devils is a God-allowing-you-to-be-tested type attack. The bottom line is this: God allows His people to be attacked so they can be tested against the temptation, tested with temptation but not go into the temptation. A temptation that God allows is only there to tune you up to be able to get through it and to be able to be made use of by the Lord Himself to help others make it through also. It is an honor to be tempted and not fail. God has chosen you to be tested. That is what the plan was all along. Yes, devils tempt, but we are never supposed to fail, not because of something we are. No, it's because of who we are in Christ. So get ready, you will be tested if you are serving the Lord. Unfortunately, the Christian world at large has been failing the test.

What are you going to do now? It will be easy to stand against the enemy now that you know Galatians 5. Easy, since Jesus paid the price. By accepting Him as Savior, you get the complete package, what you need to be holy. He gave us the Holy Spirit Who allows us to recognize the devil and not give in to the temptation. 1 Corinthians 10:13 states that the Lord always gives a way out of any and all temptation, always!

Okay, you are saying to yourself, "I have repented from anything disobedient to God. I truly want to obey Him. I choose to obey the Lord and remain a slave to righteousness." Let's look at why a servant of the Lord would be attacked by the devils. Remember, God wants you to be conformed to the image of His Son (see Romans 8:29). What is His Son? He is perfect, so God wants the same for us. God allows devils to attack you even when you are serving Him, especially when you are serving Him. It's okay; you are supposed to be tested, to pass, and not to fail.

## You Need To Know ...

### God Is Extreme Against Sin – You Must Spend Eternity Somewhere

*"And the devil, who deceived them, was thrown into the lake of burning sulfur, where the beast and the false prophet had been thrown. They will be tormented day and night for ever and ever."* (Revelation 20:10)

*"Then death and Hades were thrown into the lake of fire. The lake of fire is the second death. If anyone's name was not found written in the book of life, he was thrown into the lake of fire."* (Revelation 20:14-15)

**TOTAL VICTORY PERSPECTIVE:** ***Learn it, live it, share it!***™

## SYNOPSIS

I found out the words "perfect" and "holy" mean just that!

**Total Victory Perspective (TVP)** took the confusion out of what God expects by showing me that complete victory happened in Jesus, and now I am tempted, *not* by me, but by a Devil In Area (DIA).

The word translated "perfect" in the original Greek is *teleios*, and it means "complete, perfect, entire; without spot or blemish."

*Webster* paraphrased "perfect" as "complete in all respects, without defect."

I found out that "perfect" means what it means and "holy" means what it means: "pure, without blemish."

What does this holy stuff mean? I did not understand as I was growing up because the only teaching I ever heard was, "Yes, 'holy' means 'holy' (pure, without sin), and when Jesus said 'perfect' in Matthew 5:48, He really meant that. Peter, in 1 Peter 1:15-16, was really saying that we should 'be holy, for God is holy.' "

I believe the pastors I encountered as I was growing up were trying hard to tell people to do what is right, but their training about the sin nature still being alive in a believer limited their message to, "Try hard and good luck, but nobody's perfect!" I was told that sin still lived inside me after receiving the Spirit of God Almighty and that my evil thoughts were from my old sinful nature rising up again. I lived this way for most of my Christian life, but no more! There is victory in Jesus. I have traded the Sin/Repent Club (SRC) for the Total Victory Perspective (TVP)!

When the Lord showed me the Total Victory Perspective ... WOW! My life has been transformed! I am crucified with Christ, and I no longer live, but Christ lives in me! I am born again. I am a new creation. Now it all makes sense. I was shown by the Word and the Spirit that devils are the ones doing the tempting; it is normal to have evil thoughts come to me as a temptation; but I am free to stop at temptation and not to sin.

# PART 3

## Re-Evaluate

# CHAPTER 27

# Three Passages That Mean Total Victory

A lot of Christians question why believers cannot live out a better testimony. We are all capable of sinning, but why not stop at temptation? Hard? Yes, but not impossible. I believe there is a bigger picture of what God expects, and there is more power available to us to be able to live in victory. God supplies the deliverance that we need to be what He wants us to be.

Let's revisit three areas of Scripture and consider a more powerful interpretation than what many of us have been taught. After I reconsidered these three areas in light of total victory, the rest of the Bible makes more sense to me. Reconsidering them will not change the basic tenets of Christianity, or your salvation, or the same goal we all have in Christ, which is to live a holy life for God. I believe we are given more power than we are using.

Keep in mind that I am suggesting a reconsideration these three areas of Scripture based on my own experience at finding victory and helping boost a Christian's walk with the Lord! If you do not agree, then stay with the training you have had.

The reason I picked these three particular areas of Scripture is because they keep coming up in conversations with respect to comparing Christians to Paul's and James' writings. The perspective taught at present is: "Yes, we should be holy, but Paul and James said it is not really attainable on earth." Basically, we have been taught: "How can we expect to live a pure life if the great apostle Paul could not?"

As I researched this, with much prayer, I came to a decision. If I can look at these three areas with a perspective that gives more power to strive for holy living, then I want to go that way. This is the way I run the race in victory every moment.

If a verse can be read to mean *victory* in its translation, I have to interpret it that way. Shoot for the *victory* in Jesus, always! If in error, then let me err following what Jesus said, "Be perfect … as your heavenly Father is perfect."

I do not want to ruffle feathers. I just want to find and use every means possible to stop at the temptation every time I can. My free choice is to look at the Scriptures as *power against sin* every time. If considering verses in another perspective does not appeal to you, then don't listen to me. The bottom line is that we all are to be doing good and not evil. I believe I have found a *fast track* to holy living by considering a few Scriptures in a victory-deliverance light.

I am not saying the Bible is in error or that the writings of Paul or James are in error. NEVER! I am suggesting that we take a long hard look at what I believe these disciples were really telling us. If we can reconsider the three areas in light of total victory, it can introduce the Christian to greater holy power in which to live. As I talk with people, I am finding that others believe the same perspective I teach.

I don't know when or where biblical teaching veered from "be holy" to "sin, confess and repent." I believe the disciples and the Apostle Paul said that the old sin nature is in the past and they taught total victory. Whenever they refer to sin, it is in the past for believers, or they are referring to the lost world. I want to *not* sin! Can I not take my free choice to use God's power and stop at temptation?

We have been taught that Philippians 3 is saying that Paul has not reached holiness. "How can we really be crucified," people say, "when Paul tells us in Romans 7 that he is still struggling in sin?" Sadly, the Christian then goes forward in life and tries hard but uses a faulty premise as an excuse for failure.

As I have looked at certain Scriptures, I believe that there is greater power in Christ than that which has been translated for us by the Christian seminaries. I offer you another perspective for consideration.

Theology seems to have read the power out of what God really left us in

His Word. Total Victory Perspective (TVP) reads the power back into the Scriptures. See for yourself, and then decide.

**THE TOTAL VICTORY PERSPECTIVE:**

1. Romans 7
2. Philippians 3
3. James 1

What if we consider the possibility that we have no sin living in us after we receive the Holy Spirit? It is taught that Paul still sinned after he received Christ. If you're content with your service to God and with constantly "falling short," then do not pay any attention to what I want you to consider. Please keep serving the Lord!

This is my personal conclusion, and I ask you to just consider looking at these verses in the light of:

Lucifer—one-time sin and out,
Adam—one-time sin and out,
Jesus—one-time sacrifice to get rid of what God hates—SIN.

There are three areas of New Testament teaching that have been translated and taught that seem to lessen the victory at the cross. I used to accept the teaching that:

1. We as Christians are tempted by our own evil desires;
2. We should not fail God, but Paul was still failing, so we should not feel so bad;
3. We should keep trying, and we will grow toward being holy, but we will never actually reach holiness in this life; and
4. James was teaching Christians they still have evil living in them.

Should we limit the power Jesus gave us? No! Limited the power Jesus gave us is like driving a car only in first gear; it causes the RPMs to be maxed out quickly. You must let off the gas or the motor will blow. You can step on the gas again, but the motor will rev up only so far before you have to take your foot off the gas again. Jesus gives us everything; all gears are available, and even a turbo booster is included. We should be living a Christian life full blast, using all the gears. The Christian realm cannot live as a holy example for the world to crave if we are not using all the gears we have been given!

Let's look at another analogy. You bought a computer system with programs included that were powerful word data systems that could produce beautiful documents and professional final projects. But instead of accessing them, you only used Notepad. You worked extra hard to produce a useful document, but it was just so-so.

The person who receives Jesus is given more than just first gear or Notepad. He or she is given the holy power of God to live by. I want to wake up the Christian realm to the power we really received at the cross.

KEY TO THE UNIVERSE OF GOD: God always expects you to use your free choice to not sin. His rules have never changed. Lucifer sinned once and was instantly removed from the holy heaven, and a third of the angels were cast out with him.

After the disobedience in the Garden of Eden, the big problem in the world is sin; you have to get rid of sin to be with the Lord. God has never changed, and He never will.

First Peter 1:16 says, "Be holy, for I am holy." Meditate on 1 Peter 1:16. Notice it is written, "Be holy," not "Become holy," not "Try hard." The statement is, "Be holy." God is holy and always has expected the same of His free-choice creation. Jesus is The Way, the only sacrifice God accepts for the penalty of Adam's disobedience! Moreover, 1 Peter 1:15 says to "be holy in all your conduct."

Consider the following, keeping in mind what Jesus did with the old nature at the cross …

> *"In him you were also circumcised, in the putting off of the sinful nature, not with a circumcision done by the hands of men but with the circumcision done by Christ ..."* (Colossians 2:11)

# CHAPTER 28

## Romans 7

The following interpretation is not what the Christian realm has been taught, but consider that Paul is really relating to the past nature in Romans 7. Please do not get upset. I am not trying to change what the Bible says. I am just asking you to reread Romans 7 with the idea that Paul is relating to the old sin nature that is now crucified with Christ. Circumcision is a one-time cutting away, not a gradual removal. Crucifixion means death. If Paul is talking about the past, and he has now been totally rescued by Jesus, then "Be holy, for I am holy" is an instant possibility. We are to consider ourselves "dead to sin."

"Okay, I am dead to sin; let me go forward and serve the Lord."

"What about your old nature, Randy?"

"It is dead!"

"But what about the sin living in you?"

"Dead."

I am to be focused on stopping at temptation from a devil! Seems a lot easier to consider when I am dead to sin. The Lord is right there, waiting for me to take my free choice and use His power to *not fail* the temptation.

Consider Romans 7. Paul talks about how the Law affected the sin nature that was in him before he was born again in Christ. In Romans 7:19, he talks about his free choice under the *old* nature. When sin was still in him under the Law, even when he wanted to do good, he was compelled to do evil.

Wait! What about stopping at temptation? Because of the old sin nature living in him at that time, his nature was to sin. The Scripture shows that anyone without Christ is locked into the sin nature. Another name for it is the flesh. Jesus is your way out; receiving Him allows you to be born again spiritually. Yes, you can still fail a temptation and sin, but why fail if you can stop at temptation? If you fail the temptation, you are still saved. Repent, and next time, stop at temptation. The key is to recognize temptation, then use God's Word to do battle. In Galatians 5:19-21, there is another example of the sin nature (flesh). The old nature is against God; God gave the whole world over to this nature after Adam failed *one* time. This nature had to be crucified; it had to die.

> *"For you have been born again, not of perishable seed, but of imperishable, through the living and enduring word of God."* (1 Peter 1:23)

Romans 8 also talks about the people of the world who cannot please God. Then Paul writes that *we are not in that nature any longer because the Spirit of God now lives in us!* Verse 9 mentions the fact that, unless a person receives Christ, the sin nature will remain in them. We must take our free choice and call upon the name of Jesus to receive the *new nature*. In Christ, we are free from sin. Jesus crucified it!

> *"Those controlled by the sinful nature cannot please God. You, however, are controlled not by the sinful nature but by the Spirit, if the Spirit of God lives in you. And if anyone does not have the Spirit of Christ, he does not belong to Christ."* (Romans 8:8-9)

> *"For the flesh lusts against the Spirit, and the Spirit against the flesh; and these are contrary to one another, so that you do not do the things that you wish."* (Galatians 5:17 NKJV)

> *"So then, those who are in the flesh cannot please God."* (Romans 8:8 NKJV)

From the Old Testament all the way to the cross, all people had the sin nature (flesh). "All sinned." David also wanted to do good, but he failed because the sin nature (flesh) was not crucified in him. *Jesus*—the Lamb of God who takes away the sin of the world—*had not yet come!* Paul points out that the sin nature is always pulling a free-choice person to keep failing God.

Paul talks about the past to show how tremendously impossible it is for any to be holy without getting rid of the *sin*. The old nature had to be crucified to get us back to right standing with God.

Our wonderful Savior crucified sin, and now we are holy!

Paul is rescued by Jesus and given a new nature by the Holy Spirit. Before Jesus crucified the old nature, "Be holy, for I am holy" was extremely hard to reach because all *under Adam* had sinned and fallen short of the glory of God. Jesus crucified the sin nature. Receiving Him allows you to be given the Holy Spirit. When you are given the Holy Spirit, that is all that dwells within. The old nature is crucified, so the only nature you now have is the *new* nature from the Lord. It makes sense to me that the Holy Spirit in me is not going to share with the old nature after Jesus paid with His blood to crucify sin.

Most Christians I talk with say they still contend with an old nature and that I am wrong. If I am wrong in saying I have been crucified to sin, then I guess I will be wrong. I want to take my free choice and resist temptation by the supreme power of the Holy Spirit within me.

> *"Those who belong to Christ Jesus have crucified the sinful nature with its passions and desires."* (Galatians 5:24)

The old has been cut away.

> *"In him you were also circumcised, in the putting off of the sinful nature, not with a circumcision done by the hands of men but with the circumcision done by Christ ..." (Colossians 2:11)*

Christ lives in me, not sin. He gives us the new, the Holy Spirit. The Holy Spirit is with you and in you! You are only tempted by a devil and can stop the thought at temptation before sin. Amen!

> *"I have been crucified with Christ and I no longer live, but Christ lives in me. The life I live in the body, I live by faith in the Son of God, who loved me and gave himself for me."* (Galatians 2:20)

Praise the Lord, the new is given by receiving Christ's sacrifice!

> *"Therefore, if anyone is in Christ, he is a new creation; the old has gone, the new has come!"* (2 Corinthians 5:17)

The Holy Spirit is given to all who call upon the name of Jesus. Notice the New Testament is about the holy deliverance. After the cross, the disciples teach about how the past is gone and the new way is to stop at temptation before sin. Paul said the old has been crucified. BIG GOD little problem, and Jesus crucified the sin. After the cross, we are given 1 Corinthians 10:13 to get out of every temptation *before* sin.

> *"No temptation has overtaken you except such as is common to man; but God is faithful, who will not allow you to be tempted beyond what you are able, but with the temptation will also make the way of escape, that you may be able to bear it."* (1 Corinthians 10:13 NKJV)

We can all rejoice with Paul in Romans 7:25 when he asks the question, "Who will save me from this wretched man I am?" The answer is: JESUS!

After sin is crucified in Christ, the New Testament reports the way to live as God always intended: "Be holy, for I am holy." The world is condemned by the sin that entered after the Adamic failure. Holiness is what we are about after salvation, all the way until the last breath of life. Yes, it is a hard way to live, stopping at every temptation, but it's not impossible.

> *"But now having been set free from sin, and having become slaves of God, you have your fruit to holiness, and the end, everlasting life."* (Romans 6:22 NKJV)

# CHAPTER 29

# Philippians 3

Philippians 3 is another Scripture to reconsider. It is often taught that Paul is talking in this passage about not being holy himself when he says in verse 12: "Not that I have already attained, or am already perfected ..."

This verse has been interpreted to say that we are like the old Paul. He is not perfect, but he still strives to do right. In this instance, the word "perfected" does not mean "holy." When you understand that Paul is not talking about holiness here but is referring to the resurrection in the future of all saints, it puts more power in the fact that Jesus delivered Paul totally when Paul received Him, and we have the same total victory in Christ.

The Scripture allows us to see this in Luke 13:32. Jesus mentions the powerful event He is about to take part in after He is crucified.

> *"Go, tell that fox, 'Behold, I cast out demons and perform cures today and tomorrow, and the third day I shall be perfected.'"* (Luke 13:32 NKJV)

Jesus is certainly not saying that He is not holy but that He is going to rise on the third day, the perfected resurrection from the dead. Jesus' full purpose would not be completed until He was resurrected. The resurrection from the dead is a future event for all Christians. I love to consider total deliverance! Paul, in Philippians 3, is speaking of this future resurrection. He was living a life of holiness, and, in Christ, we can be, also!

I am asking that you look again at the whole of Philippians 3 and what

Paul is addressing. If he had been speaking of having trouble with personal holiness, I believe Paul would have said that he is not holy and needs to repent from a sin with which he still struggles. If Paul said that he cannot, in Christ, stop at temptation, we have to ask why not?

It is a lot to ponder, but what would it do to the Christian faith and our witness if these Scriptures were considered to be about sin being totally crucified in the believer? Would it hurt the faith? No! It would change the way we live by no longer thinking that we still have a sin nature with which to contend. We have now been empowered by a new "holy" nature.

Paul is telling the people in Philippi that he had not already attained his determined purpose, much like Jesus was saying in Luke 13:32. Let's look at Paul's purpose in the *Amplified Bible.*

> *"[For my determined purpose is] that I may know Him [that I may progressively become more deeply and intimately acquainted with him, perceiving and recognizing and understanding the wonders of His Person more strongly and more clearly], and that I may in that same way come to know the power outflowing from His resurrection [which it exerts over believers], and that I may so share His sufferings as to be continually transformed [in spirit into His likeness even] to His death, [in the hope] that if possible I may attain to the [spiritual and moral] resurrection [that lifts me] out from among the dead [even while in the body]."* (Philippians 3:10-11 AMP)

Paul continues his discourse in verse 12:

> *"Not that I have now attained [this ideal], or have already been made perfect, but I press on to lay hold of (grasp) and make my own, that for which Christ Jesus (the Messiah) has laid hold of me and made me His own. I do not consider, brethren, that I have captured and made it my own [yet]; but one thing I do [it is my one aspiration]: forgetting what lies behind and straining forward to what lies ahead, I press on toward the goal to win the [supreme and heavenly] prize to which God in Christ Jesus is calling us upward."* (Philippians 3:12-14 AMP)

Paul is teaching that knowing Jesus Christ intimately and understanding all that occurred in His resurrection requires progressive growth. He is striving, doing what is necessary to reach that personal goal. Frankly, there is just too much to learn about Christ and the mysteries of the cross and the resurrection for anyone to learn it all at once. A lot of that understanding will come unexpectedly through revelation by the Spirit in God's timing, if we are truly seeking it.

You will note that Philippians 3 does not mention sin, temptation, old nature, being holy, failing temptation, or repenting.

What we do need to grasp is that we *now* have, in Christ, total victory! Paul knew this and encouraged his brothers in the faith to hold true to what they had already attained and to walk and order their lives by that, rather than being swayed and turned back by those whom he called "enemies of the cross of Christ," those who side with earthly things.

What if all these years we have been missing the total message just by a little bit? Consider that someone, somewhere, years and years ago, bought into a little whisper from a devil, saying, "Did God really say be holy?" Then Scripture translation got slightly twisted and a few key areas were interpreted to discount what God expects and to water down what Jesus did on the cross.

Here is another verse on which to meditate about the word "perfected":

> *"And having been perfected, He became the author of eternal salvation to all who obey Him."* (Hebrews 5:9 NKJV)

Yes, we can repent if we sin, but why are we not looking for a way to stop at temptation every time? I believe it is primarily because of the way these three areas of Scripture have been taught—that Paul was still not holy after receiving Jesus. To say that the great Apostle Paul could not keep from failing after he received Jesus makes us say we must be the same. How then can we expect not to sin? If we believe that Paul was still sinning and not totally free from all sin, then I think we have missed Paul's message.

Jesus crucified the old nature, and we are instantly made holy by the power of the crucifixion. Paul, I believe, is stopping all sin at the temptation level, but that is not the way the scholars translate his writings. The teaching that Paul was not instantly delivered from sin to become holy became commonplace, and pastors trained in it brought what they had been taught and passed it along to their congregations. I am not putting pastors down. I am asking them to consider it from a different perspective. Why are we not training total victory in Christ? Look at these New Testament passages that can be understood as total deliverance from sin after the cross. Imagine the seminaries all over teaching the considerations I have pointed out. I believe the church would change overnight!

Jesus is the King of Kings, the Creator of all things, and the final price that was paid to "take away the sin of the world," like John reported. Jesus is all we need, and total deliverance is easier to understand as we visit Romans 7, Philippians 3, and James 1, carefully re-examining the passages we have discussed. Consider that Jesus really did crucify the old nature.

I believe neither Paul nor James was talking about a defeated Christian life whatsoever. Paul said in Philippians 3:13 that he was "forgetting those things which are behind." What was behind? His old life of sin.

Paul also referred to himself and others as being "mature" and urged those to whom he spoke to "follow his example" and to use him as a pattern for living. That certainly does not sound like a man being overtaken by sin.

Consider what I am pointing out. If you can't buy it, then don't listen to me. Regardless, please keep serving the Lord, pray for the saints, and reach out to the world with the gospel of our Lord!

Someone somewhere years ago said that those passages mean that we are still just like the world. Maybe you will prefer my conjecture that the sin nature is gone in a Christian, totally crucified! It may sound radical, but I have practiced this radical lifestyle for many years. The sin nature having been crucified in me has made it so much easier for me personally to serve the Lord. To consider all sin nature gone in me and temptation only from an outside source has enabled me to focus on the total power I believe we receive by acceptance of the awesome gift of Jesus.

I have to reaffirm that I consider Jesus the final power, and I am dead to sin.

# CHAPTER 30

## James 1

Here is an area of Scripture that I am told talks about the Christian life. If you read the start of James, you will notice he is talking to the 12 tribes that are scattered abroad. Who are these 12 tribes?

Consider that James is talking to the 12 Jewish tribes. I have had pastors tell me that James called them brethren, so they believe James is talking to Christians. If James is talking to the believers, then why did he not say "believers" or "my brethren in Christ"? If James is talking to a mixed crowd of Jews and new believers, consider the possibility that when he mentions standing and enduring temptation, he is talking to Christians. When he speaks about each one being dragged into sin by the evil within, he is talking to the ones who have not received the new nature. Read James and decide for yourself whether he is talking about the old nature controlling people *before* they receive Christ, or if he is talking to believers *after* they have received Christ.

The book of James also speaks about the sinful world and temptation by a sin nature that cannot be crucified without Christ. Notice how those people with a sin nature act: Their desires are to go with the nature of sin that lives in them. Those people, I believe, are the people of the world who are without hope unless they receive Jesus! Be a holy example for them, so they will see the deliverance Jesus gives in a lost and dying world.

> *"But each one is tempted when he is drawn away by his own desires and enticed. Then, when desire has conceived, it gives birth to sin; and sin, when*

*it is full-grown, brings forth death."* (James 1:14, 15 NKJV)

Consider the possibility that James is talking about unsaved people. The unsaved are dragged all the way down to sin, not stopping at temptation. First Corinthians 10:13 is not given to the sin-nature people. They must receive Jesus to get the new nature! They cannot stop at temptation because they are all in the sin nature, but Jesus is the way out!

It is my belief that James is showing how the old nature works; a person without Jesus has been turned over to sin. The uncrucified still have evil inside of them that entices them to sin; it is the way they are; it is their sin nature.

As followers of Jesus Christ, we need to be a holy example for the world to see because the Bible tells us that all sinners are condemned to a future of death, hell, and then the lake of fire. I believe Jesus crucified sin, and after that, we are given power by the new nature through the Holy Spirit who lives inside us to *stop* all sin at temptation. Jesus paid a one-time price, and Paul and James are telling us that the past is the past, the old nature has been crucified, and we are now holy in Christ.

Take your free choice every time you are tempted by an unholy fallen angel, and use the new nature that you received in Christ to be holy, as He is holy, and as He always requires. Use Galatians 5:19-21 to recognize with what a Devil In Area (DIA) can tempt you, and then stop before you sin! Lucifer and Adam had free choice, and God had to be extreme against sin. God sent his Son to set you free from sin, not to sin and repent, sin and repent over and over again, which is never what the Scriptures teach.

What a mind bender it is reading this perspective! Now you can see what I have been taught by the Spirit of the Lord and how extreme we can now be toward serving God. The Total Victory Perspective (TVP) has changed my life forever. I now have a mental perspective that I will have total victory against any temptation in every area of my life, and I practice this every day, every hour, every minute of my life.

I recommend that you go back and re-read this several times. Don't forget to go back to the beginning of the book and write a personal note to the Lord and sign it!

# PART 4

## Let Me Tell You A Story

# CHAPTER 31

# The Story Of A Young Christian Couple

Once upon a time, in a land too close for comfort, there was a young Christian couple, a young man and his lovely young wife. They were so young and so beautiful! The couple had only been married for a few months, and they went to church on Sundays and tried to live for God most of the time ... well, *some* of the time. They were doing the best they knew how. (The key is to do the best God knows how, but we will get to that a little later.) Their upbringing taught them that they should love God, and do what is right, but don't talk about devils because they are evil. This young couple wanted to serve the Lord and were doing the best they could, but lack of knowledge of God's Word can cause heartache and bring pain to any wonderful marriage.

Love filled the air the first few years. Then things started to get on the husband's nerves, things like the messy house. (Maybe he should be helping to keep things in order more, instead of sitting on the couch watching TV when he comes in from work.) He complained about their inexperience in handling money, working all the time, and having hardly any fun.

The wife had her flaws also, but they were less numerous. The sweet, loving couple started being contentious toward each other and, you guessed it, they yelled sometimes. Then the not-so-young-as-he-used-to-be man would leave the house and go for a drive to cool off from their little tiff. The wife, left at the house, would cry. As always the couple would kiss and make up. (Why do people say "kiss and make up"? Doesn't it seem like you would need to make up and then kiss? If you just go up to your angry spouse and plant your lips on her and she is still ticked, she might slap the presumption out of you!) Even though the couple made up, the wife, in her mind, was being told (by a devil) that the marriage was not stable. She started worrying, as if that would help anything. She started having anxiety about the future of the marriage. Because of all this wonderful advice being told to her mind, she worried and also continued to be ticked.

Meanwhile, back in the husband's mind, he is being told (by a devil), "If your wife *really* loved you, she would understand more about how much you deserve to be treated like a king. Yep, that wife is turning out to be a real pain. You can find someone who really cares for you. Surely, God wouldn't want you to be unhappy. Life is short, you probably need to face up to it—your marriage was a mistake, and you need to cut your losses and move on. Yep, you will actually be giving your wife a break by getting a divorce. It's what is best for both of you. Be a man! You can still be friends and have good wishes for each other." (Boy, this was a long-winded devil.)

Mr. Husband happens to meet a nice girl at the office. (Oh, brother, another nice, understanding woman in whom he can confide his secrets. Give me a break!) Anyway, as time goes on, the nice office girl and he start having harmless lunches together. Man, does she understand him. He also tells her, "My wife and I are not as close as we used to be." He tells her he's not sure he will even stay married, as he looks to the floor with that sad little look. A little more time goes by, and Mr. Husband finds that he is missing his office girl even while he is at his house with his wife. Whoa, hold it! The story can keep going and the situation can get even deeper, or we can simply say that this scenario is headed for even more disobedience to God.

What's really going on in this little story? Let's go to this couple's house with our *spiritual* eyes open. Before we open up the front door and enter, we will reach into our holy backpack and get a can of devil spray. (Devil spray allows the invisible devils to be seen. Wouldn't it be nice if they sold *that* at the Christian bookstore or Stuff-Mart? Devil spray, a clear, odorless environmentally friendly visualizer of evil.) Come on into the living room, and spray some devil spray over by the sofa. (Devils like to lounge around on couches, probably because their backsides are still sore from getting booted out of heaven.) As soon as the mist hits the air, there they are in our sight. Would

you look at that … three demons sitting on this couple's couch with their feet propped up on the furniture, smoking nasty cigars, spitting on the floor, and talking filth. If the husband and wife could really see this, don't you think they would tell these devils to get out of their house?

How do we keep this type of stronghold away? Let us break down what the Scriptures say, and find out how to keep the devils from getting this far.

The first mistake this couple made is noted at the beginning of our story: They do not surrender everything to the Lord. Christian marriage is a holy undertaking, and God needs to be FIRST in all things. Another big mistake is that the man has not taken his role as spiritual leader to lead his wife in the ways of the Lord so they can both share in the gift of life God has given. The two are not sold out to the Lord; therefore their focus is inexact. The man should not be counting on the pastor to give out enough of God's Word on Sunday to be enough fuel until next Sunday. The man needs to be studying God's Word for himself, and then he would know to love his wife as Christ loved the church. He gave Himself up for her. It is a big deal when the man does not to take on his proper role in the marriage. The doors are open for devils to work on changing feelings. Feelings come and go, but the Lord is constant. This couple should be serving the Lord and finding their joy in the Lord. That way, it won't matter what feeling comes to them, they will be able to rejoice because it is written to rejoice.

This couple should be studying the Word together and talking openly about their negative (devil inserted) thoughts. By reading the Word, God's Spirit can teach them about how to serve Him and how to recognize the tricks of devils. The Word freely gives us all the information we need to be able to stand against devil schemes.

Now let's take a look at how devils could have been blocked in our story.

The thought of *contention* came to their home. It is a work of the flesh (Galatians 5:19-21). The couple could have blocked that by knowing that contention has already been crucified. Those are not their thoughts. Next, they were yelling, and those are *outbursts of wrath* (Galatians 5:19-21). Those are crucified. Next the wife is feeling *anxious*, but it is not her own anxiety. The Word says, "Be anxious for nothing …" (Philippians 4:6).

What about the husband at work? Boy, a red light should have gone off in this guy's head when he saw how the devils were setting him up with the girl at the office. If this man had studied his training manual, he would have known that looking at a woman lustfully causes a man to commit *adultery* in his heart. The man had no business telling the girl at the office that he had problems with his wife. The devils have convinced this guy that it is all right to have lunch with this girl. This is the way devils can build on emotions. Speaking of emotions, look how the devils were convincing the man he had feelings for the girl at work, and he needed to miss her while at home with his wife. Oh, yeah, this guy is being set up with one of the oldest tricks in sin nature books. Sure, he thinks he misses the girl because the devils have added the sexual drive emotion into the equation. This guy is buying the thoughts

… hook, line, and sinker. The innocent friend has become an emotional goal. Sexual emotions are strong. That's why the Lord gives us a spouse to share our feelings with—not someone else. The thought this guy is getting, which is illegally energizing *sexual emotions*, is from a devil; that's how they work. The guy got the temptation and pondered it and caressed it until it is now a full-blown sin against God. (Learn to *block* when devils attack. It makes life a lot easier!)

In our little story, a lot of thoughts were injected into our loving couple. They thought they were falling out of love, and neither of them understood the other one. It looked like the best they could hope for was divorce and to get on with their own lives.

Hogwash! These thoughts are lies from devils that deceive people into believing the thoughts are their own. Devils cannot make you do anything. Their job is to convince you that the thought to disobey God is coming from you.

It is kind of like karate. In karate you are taught that when someone is about to hit you on the top of your head, you raise your arm up and block. That way your noggin doesn't get hurt. Imagine the devil with a bat … here he comes, and his plan is to knock you senseless. What will you do? You had better block right about now. You look around and say, "What, I don't see anything." About that time, BAM! Ouch, that hurts! You see, devils do not want us to realize we are in supernatural warfare. That way, what you don't know is what they use to destroy you. What liars these devils are.

God always wants His people to be holy, for He is holy, and we can do it. No devil can keep you from God. It is not that you did not want to serve God; it was that you just honestly did not know that the sin nature is dead in you, and the thoughts to disobey God are a direct devil attack. Now that you know, be on guard! Study Galatians 5:19-21, the list of acts of the sinful nature that has been crucified. Meditate on Galatians 5:22-23, the power list God gave us of fruits we can produce when we walk in His Spirit.

> *"Those who belong to Christ Jesus have crucified the sinful nature with its passions and desires."* (Galatians 5:24)

# CHAPTER 32

# The Story Of Pete And Chad

This is a make-believe story of how the realm of temptation works. A young man named Pete was sitting on his front porch one day, peacefully enjoying the beauty of the day. Pete had accepted Jesus as his personal Savior, and his free choice was to serve the Lord.

A car pulled up in front of Pete's house, and a dude got out toting something in his hand that looked like magazines. As the stranger got closer, Pete noticed that the magazines this dude had were "girlie" magazines, the sexually immoral type. Pete did not want anything to do with such magazines, nor did he want to discuss the content.

Pete knew that viewing this type of trash was against the Lord, and he wanted to obey God. Where did he stand with the Lord at this time? Pete noticed from a distance that the magazines were the disobedient-to-God-type, and he did not want to receive what the stranger was promoting.

Pete was not receiving the invitation to be involved, he was only being tempted. Because Pete rejected the temptation, he was only being tested, and because he did not sin, he does not need to repent. Pete's heart was right with God, and the Lord looked upon Pete as a man who had just passed a test. Well done, Pete!

Pete passed this part of the test by making a free will choice to obey God. God looks at the heart, and Pete wanted purity to reign. As the stranger got even closer, he said, "Hey, I'm looking to sell some sexually immoral magazines. Would you like to buy some?" (Pete saw his opportunity to spend some quality evangelism time with this guy and share with him the love of God and the truth of life. Oh, yeah, this could be a great opportunity to share Jesus! I hope he prayed and was lead to be used of God!) Anyhow, for our story, let's say the stranger's magazines were not accepted by Pete whatsoever.

Now, let's look at another young man named Chad. Chad had also received the Lord as Savior. Same scenario. Chad was outside on his porch. A stranger stopped, got out of his car, and approached Chad with sexually immoral magazines. Chad saw the sexually immoral magazines in the stranger's hand, but Chad did not turn his mind to the Lord to stop the temptation from being planted into the soil of his mind. Chad wanted to take his free choice and use it to walk the line and go for the temptation. Chad was living on the edge, and God does not like this type of behavior. Bad move, Chad.

Chad had been going to church. He knew what the Bible said about immorality, that it's a biggie with the Lord. Because Chad was receiving the thoughts injected by a devil, he wanted the stranger to let him have a look. Chad sinned against God and needed to repent and stop any further action.

Chad soiled his heart by failing the test of temptation and turning to sin. God looks at the intent of the heart, and Chad's intent was to accept the stranger's magazines. He needs to repent because he allowed the stronghold of the spiritual chains of bondage into his mind. God will forgive him, but at this point, Chad does not want to repent. As a matter of fact, he plans to buy and look at this filth. How long will it take Chad to repent? Maybe 40 years! It's not worth the sin. (The devils will waste your life, Chad! I hope he's listening.)

The same test came to both Pete and Chad. Pete called on the power of the Lord to deal with it, and Chad bought into the temptation and went deeper. After just seeing it from a distance as a temptation, he let his mind be entertained by the thoughts from devils to sin against God Almighty. That boy needs to repent. God saw both boy's intentions; you can't fool God. Pete shut it off before it could become sin, and Chad pondered and let the devil convince him to go for the lust of a nature that no longer belongs to him. Devils are liars and do not want Chad to know that the sin nature is crucified. That's their deception, and it works.

And now let's imagine the spirit realm where "we wrestle not against

flesh and blood" (Ephesians 6:10).

Pete is sitting out on his porch and thoughts come to his mind; just thoughts. Pete is sitting alone. No one (you can see) is around him. The thoughts start out, "Pete, man, do you remember the other night when you were on the Internet looking at skateboards, and there was a flashing little box that came up on screen titled "Click Here for Sexy Girls Galore," and you didn't click? What was wrong with you, Pete? (Right now, Pete is calling out, "Lord, I need your help; these are not my thoughts.") Devil in area (DIA) thoughts continue, "Think about what you could have seen! You probably blew a good chance to have some fun. Pete, man, think about that girl you saw at school yesterday. Wow! Pete, wouldn't you really like to have sex with her? Wow, Pete, think about it! You're the man, Pete. Then think about immorality. You're missing out on fun. Everybody's doing it, Pete. It's your desires that are most important. Life is short, Pete. Do something about. Be a man!"

Okay, that's enough. Thoughts are coming to Pete fast and furious. Pete, however, does not want these types of thoughts to be coming to his head. Pete is casting down the thoughts as fast as they come in because he knows these thoughts are not his. Pete honestly wants nothing to do with these thoughts. Pete wants to serve God.

It must be Pete's old sin nature telling him ... No! Jesus crucified the sin nature. It's dead. Any other guesses? I will tell you, the thoughts being injected into Pete's mind are from none other than a devil! When the thoughts came, Pete did not ponder and caress them. No, he immediately knew this was a devil attack, and Pete called upon the Lord for immediate help.

Pete is free from allowing these thoughts to go into sin, so Pete doesn't need to repent of sin because he is not allowing the thoughts to go to the next level to commit sin.

Pete knew what the Word of God says about devils' attacks, and even though you can't see the devils, Pete knew that it was a devil. Because Pete is a man of God, he has been crucified from the sin nature. Pete was not shaken by the temptation, seen or unseen. It did not matter to Pete because he knows he will be tempted in a lot of ways. These are tests to pass, not to fail. Pete strives for holiness every second of the day. Good job, Pete! Way to go! We need more young men like Pete, that's for sure.

# CHAPTER 33

# Adventures At The 437th Demon Patrol And The Prayer Of Little Suzy – A Story

Just for a moment, imagine what it would be like to address General Demon and Sergeant Devil. Imagine what it would be like to go behind the scenes to the enemy's camp to see and hear what really goes on. Before we go, though, let's go over a few of the rules to the game, both in this story *and* in real life. Devils have to abide by God's rules, and the more you know how the rules work they are all in the Bible—the better off you will be.

Here are some of the things God allows devils to do: In a believer's life, a devil can only tempt. We know that temptation is not sin, but acting on the temptation *is* sin. When a believer sins against God, that gives devils the ability to put a spiritual ball and chain on the leg of the believer. (*This* you do *not* want!) If the believer does not repent, the ball and chain remain.

Devils may hang around and keep tempting, not only with the evil they originally used against a believer, but with other temptations that are deceptions. Never does a believer have to give in to the temptation, but the demons always know where the believer is most vulnerable. It just doesn't make any sense to have a relationship with the hateful devils when the believer has the Spirit of God within.

Devils tempt believers, but believers can always say no. If a believer does sin, then they have given rights to a devil that allows that devil to stay around and keep that same temptation coming. The devil deceives the believer to receive the temptation as his or her own thought and sin against God over and over. God allows the temptation, but the believer is not ever supposed to follow through to sin. (See 1 Corinthians 10:13.)

A non-believer is still living in the old sinful nature; he or she has not accepted God's free gift of salvation. Non-believers have not repented from sin and received Jesus as Savior, so God's wrath remains on them.

A non-believer operates in the sin nature, and so do devils! Devils have an easy task with non-believers because non-believers do not have the Spirit of God living in them. Devils simply manipulate the non-believer to do more evil. Devils are allowed to operate in the sin realm, and a non-believer is in the sin realm. He or she will do what the sin nature directs against God. Devils don't have a tough job getting non-believers to do evil. It is already the non-believer's nature! Devils don't have to mess with them much at all; they are already lost. And the deception encourages ever-escalating evil in the life of a non-believer.

What if you could see behind the scenes? Maybe it would be something like the following story.

## The 437th Demon Patrol Headquarters

SETTING: The scene is a military-type office; the lighting is low. At the back wall facing away from us, in the center of the room, is a large leather chair, and it is rocking back and forth slowly with a slight creak. With each movement of the chair, we hear a raspy breathing sound coming from someone sitting there. As we slowly and cautiously look around the dimly lit office, we notice a plaque on the wall to the left of the chair. The plaque is inscribed:

**General D. Zalk**
437th Demon Patrol
In appreciation
for all your murderous accomplishments
for the destruction of human lives
in the 437th district
this plaque of gratitude
*(I can almost make out the last line. It says …)*
Satan, Prince of Darkness

(Suddenly, there is a knock, knock, knock on the door. The chair spins around, and we see the one sitting there. He is a being about four feet tall, wearing a military type uniform complete with ribbons and medals, the kind that are given for success in missions. His name badge displays "Zalk." The creature has green glowing eyes, and a light burgundy shade of skin. His hands are covered with small scales that overlap down to his fingers. The nails are two-inch claws.)

(Knock, knock, knock at the door again.)

GENERAL: "Come in."

(The general lights up a fresh cigar. The door opens and in steps another being, also in military dress, but with hardly any medals or rank symbols except a few stripes on the shoulder of his jacket. This being is also around 4 feet tall, but his skin is light green.)

"Ah, Sergeant Dufer."

SERGEANT: "Yes, sir, General, sir. Sergeant Dufer reporting from demon Sector 382, Quadrant X3 and Z4, sir."

GENERAL: "At ease, Sergeant. I am General Zalk, and I will be handling your review. Come in and have a cigar. They are the nastiest I can find and leave a terrible aftertaste in your mouth."

SERGEANT: "Thank you, General; and may I say that your office smells like a pig's behind and an overflowing sewer."

GENERAL: "Don't flatter me, boy! Just have a seat, and let's get down to business."

SERGEANT: "You are extremely kind to offer me your very worst! Thank you, sir."

(There is a solemn smirk on the general's face as he looks at the sergeant. Sergeant Dufer reaches out to take the stogie, bites off almost half of it and swallows. He then lights up the other end, and smoke fills the air. He is very nervous.)

GENERAL: "Have a seat, Sergeant. Okay, let me explain a few things. Major Billo of your sector was sent on special assignment, so I am the one who will be conducting your evaluation at this time."

(The general opens a folder.)

"The review will consist of questions prepared for all Level-4 devils from:

• the Bible,
• Basics of Deception Protocol (BDP),
• Demon Doctrine and Rules (DDR), and
• Strategic Satanic Deception Manual (SSDM).

You will be administered the standard questions from Demon Doctrine and Rules (DDR) and then allowed to answer. Next, because you are trying for a promotion to Level 5, you will be administered questions from the Strategic Satanic Deception Manual (SSDM). After all questions and answers are completed, we will explore your personal sector productivity. All information will be graded by administration and set before the Board of Requests. The Board will evaluate the approval or disapproval of your present position, advancement or, my favorite, immediate demotion. The complete evaluation and end result decision will take approximately eight weeks. Any questions?"

(The general did not even give the sergeant time to respond when he answered his own question.)

"Good, let's begin. In the Bible, what verse or partial verse can devils use to tempt a new believer to fall back into sin?"

SERGEANT: "That would be in Romans: 'All have sinned and fall short of the glory of God.'"

GENERAL: "And what thought injection could be added for the kill?"

SERGEANT: "Tell the new believer they are only human, and God will forgive them when they sin, so it's okay to fail because God knows they are not perfect."

GENERAL: "From Demon Doctrine and Rules, Paragraph 4C, what is the best way to have humans think about Satan?"

SERGEANT: "As the guy with the red suit, pitchfork, and horns."

GENERAL: "Sergeant, from the Strategic Satanic Deception Manual, page 666, Paragraph 8C, what is suggested to distract young men at church?"

SERGEANT: "That would be having girls dress inappropriately at church. This allows lust demons authority over the men who succumb to the temptation to sin."

GENERAL: "What can a devil inject into a believer's mind when they are told, 'Be holy, for I am holy'?"

SERGEANT: "Tell them that it is *impossible* to do. Only Jesus is holy, and they are not Jesus."

GENERAL: "What Basic Deception Protocol (BDP) is used to poison the mind of a non-believer when they are introduced to John 3:16, 'For God so loved the world that He gave His only begotten Son that whosoever believes in Him should not perish but have everlasting life'?"

SERGEANT: "Get them to think that the word 'believe' means 'an intellectual understanding that Jesus was a great prophet on earth.' Also, have them not relate to 'everlasting' except as a fairy-tale-type farce."

GENERAL: "From Strategic Satanic Deception Manual (SSDM), what is one of the best ways to describe God so as to not give Him any deity?"

SERGEANT: "That would be to address Him as something casual like, 'The Man Upstairs.' "

GENERAL: "Sergeant, from the Demon Doctrine and Rules, Paragraph 4B, when a non-believer is starting to ask too many questions of a believer, what can be done to steer them away from being saved?"

SERGEANT: "Okay, you said Paragraph 4B … Ugh! Oh, the answer is to bring them into contact with some believers who are compromising their walk, using the double standard of saying one thing but doing another …"

GENERAL: "Be more specific, Sergeant. What do you mean? Give me three deceptions and examples."

SERGEANT: "Three? Okay, that's easy: 1) The first deception would be *hatred.* Example: Have non-believer placed around a believer who says he can't stand someone at his own church! 2) The second deception is *immorality.* Example: Place the non-believer in an area where the believer is one who brings a Bible to work and reads on breaks, but that same believer tells dirty jokes to fellow employees. 3) The third deception is *envy.* Example: Have the non-believer hear a believer say that he envies the size of another church member's home. Have him also say that he deserves that kind of home, and that other person does not."

GENERAL: "That's good. I did notice, Sergeant, that you picked out the church members as bad examples. Very good! In a lot of cases, that's true. We should always take advantage of compromising believers to show the deception in this Jesus stuff. Make church attendance look just like joining a country club. Have them believe there is really no difference.

Sergeant, from the Demon Doctrine and Rules (DDR), Paragraph 7A, what tool is essential in deceiving Christians to compromise?"

SERGEANT: "That answer is secular movies and music."

(The communication link rings and the general answers on the speaker.)

GENERAL: "I am in a review and left instructions I was … (raising his voice) … NOT TO BE INTERRUPTED EXCEPT FOR EMERGENCIES!"

SECRETARY: "Yes, General, an emergency *has* come up in Demon Sector 383 on the Larry Wilman account."

GENERAL: "What about him?"

(As the general eats a big chunk of the fire end of his cigar, his attitude is heating up!)

SECRETARY: "I have Major Lotar, the major of the Demon Sector 383, on line 3. Will you talk with him? He is really going up the wall, he doesn't …

(The general interrupts with disgust in his voice.)

GENERAL: "Put the stupid loser on!"

(The general types on some keys and pulls up the 383 Wilman file.)

MAJOR: "General, regarding Demon Sector 383, there are a lot of believers who will be praying for the atheist society rally one week from Friday. Demon Sector 383 specialists found out that an old friend of Larry Wilman's named Terry Butler got saved, and he plans to share his new faith with Wilman. These men were good devil puppets when they were in college together. These guys were straight-laced, non-smokers, non-cussing, non-drinkers and even helped organize marathon runs for cancer research and promoted blood drives for their college. Butler and Wilman were intellectual, nicely dressed young men headed for hell. We loved these guys! Selfish ambition caused them to deny God because we had devils tell them there is no God, only this life. They believed they didn't need that religion crutch, only their minds. For 17 years, they both have been moving forward on their atheist teaching and have been useful in helping send many to darkness.

(The general looks over to Sergeant Dufer.)

GENERAL: "This won't take but a minute, son, then we can continue your review."

(Sergeant Dufer nods his head in agreement. Major Lotar continues talking on the speaker.)

MAJOR: "Also, General, Wilman's second cousin is a real pain in the neck. She keeps praying for Wilman and talking that Jesus trash at every family get-together. Our evaluation of past events with this type of scenario shows that this situation can cause a man to cave in and listen to the best friend!"

(The general is listening, completely relaxed. He lights up another cigar and rolls his eyes up toward the ceiling. The major continues with excitement in his voice!)

"This could be devastating because we really need Wilman; he must remain unsaved! This news could maybe shake Wilman into being a Christian. What do we need to do, General? What do we tell the 383 demon sergeant and soldiers on patrol?"

(General takes a puff from his cigar and straightens a few papers on his desk.)

GENERAL: (Nonchalantly.) "Kill Wilman."

MAJOR: "What? General, Wilman is doing great damage for us!"

GENERAL: (Calmly.) "You question me?"

MAJOR: "No, sir."

GENERAL: "Have him murdered tonight; that will send him to hell!"

MAJOR: "As you command, General!"

(A moment of silence.)

"Beg your pardon, sir, but what about the atheist meeting?"

GENERAL: "Not to worry. Wilman's brother, Frank, will take over. He hates Jesus just as much, and because he is rude to Christians, hardly any are praying for him. Frank even looks evil with those tattoos and that hairstyle. He throws believers off guard; they are instantly judging him by appearance, thus not sending out any prayers for him. The records show devils are tempting believers to hate him, and they are committing the sin of hatred! We don't have to be concerned for now about him getting close to a believer and listening. Frank is serving Satan whole-heartedly; he believes in himself and is ready to move into his brother's position. No one will miss Wilman; his usefulness is finished. Just look at the charts, Lotar. Wilman's charts show angelic activity has increased around him. He has too many praying for him to take any chances. The risk is too high. If he becomes saved, he can destroy the deception of thousands. Kill him now! Will there be anything else, Major Lotar?"

MAJOR: "No, sir. Thank you, sir. Major Lotar, signing off."

(The general turns off the COM link switch and looks over to Sergeant Dufer.)

GENERAL: "Sorry about the interruption. Those demons should know when disposal of humans is due. Lost humans are a dime a dozen; never hang on too long when they are being prayed for that much. Most Christians don't pray for atheists, so we usually leave them around for a while as long as damage is occurring on a monthly basis. It is best to just cut your losses and move on to the next person if Christians are continuing to focus prayer on one particular individual. Now back to your review, Sergeant Dufer. The next portion of the review is your sector performance. Give me a report about Quadrant Z4 of …"

(He hesitates and looks over at his screen.)

"… Sector 382."

SERGEANT: "Abortion is at an all-time high."

(Sergeant takes a puff of his cigar and chokes a little.)

GENERAL: "Good."

SERGEANT: "Marriages are turning to divorce at a rate of over fifty percent."

GENERAL: "Uh huh."

SERGEANT: "Rape and murder are doing exceptionally well, and hatred between the races and/or a mix of religious hatred has exceeded our fondest hopes. Did I mention the ever increasing use of pornography, even among church officials? The Internet allows access in the privacy of one's office."

(Sergeant clears his throat from cigar choking earlier.)

GENERAL: "Very impressive."

SERGEANT: "Yes, overall we demons in Sector 382 have been wreaking havoc all around our domain. We have been expanding the evil acts of the lost and successfully disarming the testimonies of the so-called believers of Jesus the Savior, our Enemy. Like we like to say at Sector 382, 'rich or poor, we'll stomp them to the floor.' "

GENERAL: "That's catchy."

SERGEANT: "Oh yes, with all the distrust, hatred, and immoral lifestyles, we are definitely winning this war. And that's in the Christian realm."

(Both laugh.)

"General, I really thought that after Christ ..."

(Both spat on the floor out of disrespect to His name.)

"... crucified the sin nature, with which the whole world had been cursed after our dark leader deceived Adam and Eve in the garden, well, sir, I figured it was going to be a rough time convincing believers to disobey God."

(Both demon and devil recite in unison.)

"We deceive, they believe."

"But it's so simple, General. They still think that the thoughts in their minds are from the old nature. Man, when that sin nature got crucified at the cross, I figured that was it for us. I mean, what power were we going to have against those believers who are crucified at the cross? It was a real hectic time after that resurrection day!"

"Wow, General, the whole underworld was shaken to the core. Yet, I never will forget what the prince of darkness said after that day. Satan reminded us that the humans still can't see us, so we have it made. Our business is deception. Deception, oh, what a powerful tool the prince of darkness has given us! Believers think the thoughts of sinning against God are their own."

(Both laugh.)

"General, it's like taking candy from a baby."

(About this time, the sergeant is becoming more comfortable with the situation.)

(Whispering, he leans closer to the general's desk.)

"Hey, General, you ever wonder about the next event?"

GENERAL: "Next event?"

(Eyebrows pushed down in a confused look.)

"What event, Sergeant?"

SERGEANT: (Still whispering.) "You know, General, whenever the rapture of the church …"

(The general comes up out of his chair, his voice raised in anger!)

GENERAL: "Stop right there! You can't ask such questions; you are *never* to question the authority of Satan!"

(He slams his hand on the table!)

"He got us this far. You can count on him to come up with some even better deception that will carry us on and on! Don't ever talk to me or any devil about doubting the future leadership!"

SERGEANT: "Sorry, General. I will never mention it again. You are right. Thanks for your vast depth of knowledge. It has steered me clear already. Forget such nonsense! Yes, I have already forgotten … what were we talking about?"

(The general sits back down. The sergeant looks around the office frantically, trying to change the subject fast!)

"Wow, General, what is that medal?"

(He points to the general's jacket.)

GENERAL: (Loudly!) "Never mind that! Let's get back to your review."

SERGEANT: "No, really, General, that medal makes you look really powerful, and …"

GENERAL: "Boy, don't try to snow …"

SERGEANT: "No, really, I never saw one like that."

(As a feeling of pride begins to rise in the general, he leans back in his chair with a look of disgust and irritation.)

GENERAL: "Sergeant, that medal is for three-generation destruction."

SERGEANT: "Wow! Oh, yeah, now I remember! I heard that a few high monarch demons accomplished that back in … uh … but this is the first time I've actually seen one."

(The sergeant reaches out his hand to the general. The general slaps the sergeant's arm away. Still trying to convince the general he is sincere …)

"May I say, General, congratulations. And may I take a closer look at that magnificent tribute to your accomplishments?"

GENERAL: (Suspicious but prideful.) "Go ahead and take a look."

(As the sergeant draws closer to the medal, he sees the number 75/3 engraved in the middle of the medal. The sergeant ponders to himself for a moment.)

SERGEANT: "That's when a demon can deceive and maintain 75% of a family for three generations right into hell. Oh, yeah, abortion can count as the murder you need to qualify."

GENERAL: "Right. Now sit back down, and let's get back to your review."

(General takes another puff of his cigar.)

SERGEANT: "Wow, General! 75%! What a deal! It must have taken a lot of … uh."

GENERAL: (With irritation in his voice.) "Determination and hard work. That's what it takes, determination and hard work. Now, stop with the interruptions and let's see how much work you have been up to."

"Sergeant, it is our duty to keep the believers in the dark, to never let them know that it's our thoughts injected into their minds that cause them to use their free choice to go our way."

SERGEANT: "Disobedience always brings in condemnation. We are duping these believers right and left. They don't realize our existence in their lives because they can't see us."

GENERAL: "Yes, it is a wonderful deception. Make sure you keep the extra attack Special D Forces on families and any pastors and/or associates of churches who say publicly that they want to live for Jesus Christ."

SERGEANT: "Yes, sir, we are here to steal, kill, and destroy. That's Scripture, you know."

GENERAL: (Snaps!) "Yes, I know Scripture! Speaking of that, are you conducting the daily Bible study with your small group of devils? The more Scripture you can remember, the better off you will be to misquote and take God's Word out of context."

(The sergeant is looking around the room at the walls filled with awards and trophies.)

SERGEANT: "General, your awards your trophies … man, are you one *bad* devil!"

(The general knows he is great at his position and always shows great pride in his accomplishments.)

GENERAL: (Interrupting.) "Enough with the pleasantries, Sergeant Dufer. Give me an update on …"

(The general looks down at his desk at a list.)

"… on the final outcome from the emergency in Quadrant X3."

(Silence fills the room for a few seconds, and then the sergeant speaks.)

SERGEANT: "General, sir, I am not aware of any X3 problems."

GENERAL: (Shouting!) "What?"

(The general leaps to his feet and places both hands on his desk, claws scratching the wood. Sergeant Dufer is frozen in his chair and looks at the general with total confusion, not saying a word.)

(Screaming!) "You didn't get a copy? How can that be? Let me show you what you missed, you idiot!"

(The general slaps at some device and presses a button that ejects some papers.)

"Here, Sergeant!"

(The general forcefully shoves the paper into the sergeant's hand. The sergeant takes the paper and quickly looks intently at it, his eyes scanning quickly.)

"Well?"

SERGEANT: "It's a picture of an old lady. And may I add, she's an ugly one."

GENERAL: (In a low growl). "Remove your hand from the bottom of the page."

SERGEANT: (Screaming!) "Ahhhh! This is no old lady; this is a praying grandmother! Excuse me, General!"

(The sergeant's cigar drops from his lap, then to the floor, and he rises quickly and stomps it out. Then the sergeant reaches for his tele/px/ceiver and presses some numbers. The general is looking on with extreme disgust on his face. The sergeant starts making commands to someone on the other end.)

"All X3 and X4 officer destruct forces and dark mate five and six respond to a Level 6 at T-5 and intercept with all exception grid 2077 matrix. This is an order!"

(Then Sergeant Dufer looks at the general, and a small smile sneaks over his features.)

"General, I don't know what to say! I don't know how this got overlooked. Uh … it will be taken care of immediately."

GENERAL: (Yelling!) "It better be, or else I will personally see to it you are sent to a country where they don't believe in God at all!"

SERGEANT: (In a voice filled with fear.) "Oh, not *that*, general! That would be no challenge because they are already lost. A demon has to wreak havoc! It's our life! Please, give me another chance. I assure you, you can relax; the problem is now being handled by my best destroyers!"

(The general is still outraged and is speaking loudly.)

GENERAL: "How did this slip through to this level? Did you not put sickness and disease on the old lady? It is required; as stated in the Strategic Satanic Deception Manual (SSDM), Paragraph 4, Section 6, Subsection R, and I quote …"

SERGEANT: (Interrupting.) "I know, General. Yes, sir, we did afflict her with heart problems and also arthritis."

GENERAL: "And?"

SERGEANT: "And that's as close as we could get with so many people in her life praying and bringing in those big angels. Anyway, General, the old lady went to church, and the elders prayed the arthritis away. She still has the heart problems, and I'm sure the old hag will die off soon."

(The general still looks steamed.)

"Don't worry, General. I have it under control. Don't worry at all. I have the strongest demons in the area on the case. I really have it under control!"

(The general sits back in his chair and speaks with a normal tone of voice.)

GENERAL: "You realize that Satan himself is supposed to come here. Son, do you have any idea what this kind of foul-up can cause in my ranks? I am one of the finest generals anywhere. I have been awarded a number of times for my work, and I really like being first. Do you realize, boy, that I alone control forces in excess of 10 million demons? You stupid devil, this is not acceptable at all! My future and status are at stake here, and no little half-wit sergeant is going to cause me to lose any of my promotions!"

(General takes a bite of his cigar and shortens it to half.)

SERGEANT: "I understand, General. I would not want to be the cause of any problems in your division, and as I said, my best devils are on the job! You will have a complete report, General, that fully outlines all details of the complete ordeal, with names of any demons who are responsible and any protocols that were not followed. Everything will be addressed and individuals will be reprimanded."

GENERAL: "Okay. I will give you 13 hours. That's 13 hours, or we will have a serious talk about where your future demotion will take you!"

(The general takes a big bite of the cigar, chews thoughtfully, and then eats the fire. He settles back down in his chair again.)

"Sergeant, I used to work with some of your relative demons from before the garden. When I was new at the game, they helped me out, so I kinda owe them a favor. (With hesitation in his voice.) I will give you your chance, boy."

SERGEANT: "Thanks, General. It really means a lot to me. Really, thanks."

(There is silence for a few seconds, and then the general speaks in a low voice.)

GENERAL: "This could wind up like the tracker demon problem that happened last year in Sector 383. But, of course, you remember that incident. It was in all the headlines of Daily Demon News."

(Taking his pen in hand to continue the review, the general is about to write on the sheet.)

"One sector away from you, Sergeant. How did it make you feel?"

(The general lights up another fresh cigar. There is a moment of silence, and then the sergeant looks at some pictures on the wall.)

SERGEANT: "I see you have a picture of Hitler. He was a pretty bad dude, huh?"

(He is *desperately* trying to get the general to talk about something else.)

GENERAL: "Sergeant Dufer, don't tell me …"

SERGEANT: "Okay, no! I don't recall the 383 incident, General."

(The general's eyes are glowing a bright green.)

GENERAL: "What? How could that get by you, Sergeant? Tell me that! It was a massive foul-up, and many demons lost positions! Everybody knew about it!"

(The sergeant looks dumbfounded and cringes.)

SERGEANT: "I am so occupied with, uh, Sector 382 that I hardly ever get to cross sector lines to share in strategies. I attend any quarterly tactic meetings, of course, except my own Sector 382. Did I say that right?"

(The sergeant is fumbling for words. After a few seconds of silence, the general is showing his disgust.)

"Tell me what happened, General. I really want to know. That is, sir, I *need* to know! *Please*, General … I … uh … would really appreciate it."

(The sergeant is sitting up in his chair and trying to look very sorry and sincere. The ol' general takes a puff of his cigar and leans back into the cushion of his fine leather chair. There is such a silence in the room that you can hear a flame crackle from the corridors of hell. The general is disgusted but begins to tell the story.)

GENERAL: "There was a close call in the realm of darkness last year, for sure, Sergeant, and the missed destruction was almost fulfilled in Sector 383. Quadrant F could have been set back for decades. The block that was done was still not as successful as first planned. It is now history, so the most we can do is learn from the mistakes that were made and not repeat them next time."

SERGEANT: "Sounds big, General. Tell me more."

(The sergeant is just relieved that the general is talking again.)

GENERAL: "There was a young couple, both in their late twenties. They were going to church but were not really giving all their lives to follow Jesus Christ. They had a baby girl, little Suzy. When the child was around two years of age, an elderly widow at church bought one of those storybook picture Bibles and gave it to the couple as a Christmas present. The book sat around for about six months, and dust began to collect on it. We even had a low rank demon shove some other books over it so it would be hard to find. Those easy-to-follow picture Bibles can be disastrous to our cause of deception for destruction of human lives.

"Prayer was going forth from the meddling old widow. She prayed specifically for the picture Bible to be read to little Suzy. God sent angels to uncover the book. We could not get in when the angels were sent to protect the holy little family; what a pain.

"A few days went by, and one night the father was going to read some fairytale story to Suzy when he looked over by her nightstand and found the storybook Bible. The Spirit of God spoke to the father's heart, whispering for him to pick up the Bible and read it to the little girl. The elderly widow kept praying every day for the couple to read the Bible to Suzy and for her to be saved. To make a long story short, the couple began reading the picture Bible to Suzy every night, and when she was six years old, she asked Jesus to come into her heart."

SERGEANT: "Yuck! What about taking out the old widow, General? Why couldn't the demons take out the old widow?"

GENERAL: "Too much dedication in the old widow. She kept a life of continual prayer for a hedge of protection. The old widow asked God to use her to be a prayer warrior and an intercessor for the saints. This old hag was a real pain in the pitchfork, if you know what I mean. This type of dedicated servant is extremely hard to deceive because so many angels were surrounding her protecting her from us."

SERGEANT: "Man, General, this sounds like an impossible defeat. What happened next?"

GENERAL: "Finally, the old widow died off."

SERGEANT: "Great!"

GENERAL: "Yes, we were finally through with having to try to deceive her to lighten up on the prayers so we could whip in a sickness, maybe get her not to go to church anymore. The funeral was sickening; the pastor told of the love of Jesus and reassured everyone there that if they would ask Jesus into their heart, like the loving saint widow, they also could be saved. He added more garbage like that and asked the people to pray to receive Jesus. Two men who were the widow's grandsons came forward. The grandsons said they always saw a difference in their grandmother's life and knew that they needed to get right with God. The men said they figured that there was plenty of time, so they brushed off what their grandmother told them about their need to receive Jesus and live for God. Yes, Sergeant, I hate these kinds of funerals, where they turn death into an opportunity to receive life in Jesus. Yuck! It was really hard for a devil to stay around, especially when the men told the pastor that they felt something pulling them that day to come to the pastor and have him pray with them to receive this free gift that granny was always talking about. Those men prayed and got saved."

SERGEANT: "Why all this talk about these grandsons? Where do they fit in about little Suzy?"

GENERAL: "On the night before the meddling old granny died, she got her grandsons together and told them about all the people she was praying for and how she wanted to, if you will, pass the list on to them."

SERGEANT: "What a sneaky dog this granny was! Man, the nerve of that woman!"

GENERAL: "The grandsons, out of respect, actually got a note pad and wrote down the list of people dear granny had been praying for and …"

SERGEANT: "Let me guess, General. Little Suzy was on the list."

GENERAL: "You got it, Sergeant. A little annoying pain in the pitchfork—makes me sick to think about—Suzy. The granny prayed with her grandsons and asked God to keep blessing her request and for her grandsons to receive Jesus as their Lord and Savior. What a kick in the teeth! Like I said, at the funeral, the grandsons prayed to receive Christ into their hearts. It was that hogwash that the pastor spewed that day about *'if you want to see your granny again someday,'* they would need to be saved by the blood of Jesus. We just needed a few days to go by for the grandsons to mourn the old hag's passing, and then they could misplace the dangerous note pad or better yet, throw it into the trash by accident …"

SERGEANT: "Accident, my foot …"

(Both laugh.)

GENERAL: "Yes, Sergeant, you're right. It would be no accident; that note pad would be devastating to the powers of darkness. The plan was to get a Level 5 demon to find the opportunity to slip the note pad into an old daily newspaper that would be thrown into the trash. Sergeant, we kept those grandsons in the dark all their lives. One was 38, and the other was 42 years old."

SERGEANT: "What a bum deal."

GENERAL: "The bottom line here, Sergeant, was that the grandsons were now seriously reading the list and praying for the people. That meant more prayer for little Suzy, and that brought more power and protection for the little boy Suzy would bring into her little prayer realm the following week. The little boy happened to live in a country where we had been keeping a stronghold on a devil-controlled man by the name of President Joseph Mantre."

SERGEANT: "Who's President Mantre?"

GENERAL: "We'll get to him shortly. Let's get back to Suzy and the family. Things were really beginning to fall apart for the powers of darkness; it did not look good for us at all. Little Suzy's prayers over Mommy and Daddy were blocking our attempts at destruction. Oh, the power that a little child has, to ask God for all kinds of things. He always answers quickly. The action broke wide open one night. You see, because of the angelic stronghold from the prayers of the widow's grandsons, combined with Suzy's family praying … Well, you just can't be too careful in a situation like that. Very volatile, hard to predict the next move of the angels. God was honoring the prayers, and people kept praying, and praying, and praying. It's enough to make a demon sick.

"We had a Lieutenant Blaydor and his devils on station at Suzy's house, patrolling the area. Lieutenant Blaydor of Sector 383 had somewhat planned ahead because of the prayers, but not soon enough for what was going to happen on the night of February 23. The lieutenant was definitely missing something. I have had some trouble with that lieutenant on following destruction order and rank 6 protocol key elements to break into a couple's life for destruction. Sector 383's medium level devils were on patrol that night when the sneaky little brat, Suzy, prayed a prayer that moved in a great multitude of angels. Yes, a great number of angels were sent to … well, more on that later."

SERGEANT: "What happened next, General? Tell me. This story is getting extremely exciting, but it looks like we're going to be losing this little battle."

GENERAL: "We didn't lose completely; there were some good hits on our side. But let me continue with the story. A vital lesson in tactics is here for you to learn. Pay attention to what happens next."

SERGEANT: "Okay, General, it's good to know that we didn't lose. I was really thinking that, with all that was going on, we must have. Please do go on with the story."

(The general takes another puff of his nasty cigar and continues the story.)

GENERAL: "You see, on the night of February 23, Suzy and her family were watching TV, and one of those special Christian outreach programs came on. It was the kind that shows the poor starving little children who need you to send money to help. Suzy saw a pitiful looking little boy about five years old and asked her daddy, 'Can't we sponsor some child, Daddy? Wouldn't God want us to help?' Her dad and mother agreed and made the phone call to the organization and pledged to sponsor a child."

SERGEANT: "That's not too bad. What's the big deal? Why did that shake the 383rd Sector?"

GENERAL: "It wasn't that sponsoring a little child was destroying our plans; it was what happened next. A rank 6 demon caused the TV reception to go out, but it was not soon enough. This is where I believe the lieutenant made his worst mistake; *he* should have ordered the disabling of the TV signal when he saw that the little girl had compassion in her heart for the suffering people in those poor countries. The dad tried to fix the TV, and angels were fighting the demons that were over by the TV. By the time he got the station to come in, the program was going off. The situation went from bad to worse when that sneaky little brat, Suzy, asked her daddy if she should pray for the poor little boy she saw on TV.

So she prayed, and two angels threw a demon out the back door at that prayer! There were also angels there that night keeping some of the demons pinned to the garage area because of the prayers of the family. Lieutenant Blaydor didn't request any new troops in at that time; he just stood there and watched. Stupid! So the demons at Suzy's house were not told to do anything extra. Everything looked like it was staying the same. Also, the number of angels there did not change."

This was really a project for a more experienced demon, but with all the overtime projects occurring due to some Christians standing against us, Blaydor was all we could get at that time for Sector 383. The lieutenant was not following protocol. Section 21, Paragraph 4 states 'distant prayers from one country to another country determined to be on behalf of or in conjunction with fellow parties or someone else in principle locations or prompting said parties to action are always to be considered a cause of and/or can constitute a serious threat to demonic opposition and/or force heaven-sent messengers of intervention, thereby providing for the protection of the above-mentioned prayed-for party from demonic attack.' "

SERGEANT: "Yes, General, it's been a while since I read that particular part of Demon Doctrine and Rules (DDR). Could you translate for me? What the heck does all that jargon really mean?"

GENERAL: (Raising his voice in disgust!) "You should take more time to learn our rule book! How do you expect to advance if you don't know all the deceptive ways of darkness? For the sake of time, I'll tell you what Paragraph 4 means. The bottom line is that any time a child is praying earnest prayers to God, and a lower Level 6 demon sees a directly connected prayer specifically for a stranger, the demon is supposed to report the prayer and send out a rank 7 or 8 medium demon (known as a tracker devil) to respond. Always! You can never, let me repeat, *never*, know what a child can bring forth in God's protection as they ask him to help someone else. The key point was that Suzy was praying unselfishly for the little boy. That type of prayer constitutes a rank 7 or 8 because of the words 'someone else' in the first part of Paragraph 4. This is an extremely dangerous prayer against the dark forces. Extremely! Let me show you how this little mistake escalated to a RED ALERT Level 6."

SERGEANT: "A RED ALERT Level 6, General? I thought Red Alert Level 6 was for multitude involvement of thousands and above."

GENERAL: "Yes, you are right, and here is how the multitude of angelic involvement occurred. As you recall, Sergeant, I talked about Suzy praying for the poor little foreign boy?"

SERGEANT: "Yes."

GENERAL: "That little menace, Suzy, prayed for the little boy to be fed and clothed and for him to have someone to tell him about Jesus. The part of the world the little boy was in was thousands of miles away in Sector 8709, and the demons of that area were keeping the people poor by increasing greed in the government officials and in the country's leader, President Joseph Mantre.

"Remember that I spoke earlier of President Joseph Mantre. Now let me fill you in on this man's background. Yes, President Mantre of the country Pelomia was a deceptive, greedy, backstabbing, murderous, hateful leader. You'd really like him! Mantre was making deals to sneak in nuclear weapons, and he was crazy enough that he was going to actually launch the weapons at neighboring countries, even though it would kill millions of his own people. Yes, President Joseph Mantre was indeed a mentally twisted individual. Mantre even had chemical weapons that he was planning to use on his own people within the next 6 months. Part of the plan that Mantre had was to stage a fake skirmish that would make it appear that a neighboring country, Zeltonia, wanted to engage in violence against Pelomia. President Mantre was power-hungry and was planning mass destruction. Yes, we were so proud to have such an evil man in charge of the country! Mantre cared only about himself; he never received Jesus as Lord, so the sin nature was at its best. Demons had it made in the area. Hardly anything to do except keep out anyone who would teach about God. The sin nature makes our job so easy. The non-saved are already in it, and our forces of darkness deceive the saved people into thinking they are, too."

SERGEANT: "Wow! It sounds like everything was going good for our side."

GENERAL: "Not so fast! Here's what happened. A big problem was that God was honoring little Suzy's prayers. Let me tell you, God was honoring little Suzy's prayers to such an extreme that so many angels were called to station, and other angelic groups came in by the multitudes. Remember that there was still the same number of angels at little Suzy's house. Yes, indeed, the power of little Suzy's prayer caused God to send forth a multitude of angels on her behalf alright!"

SERGEANT: "Wait a minute, General. I thought you said the number of angels at her house didn't change."

GENERAL: "Exactly! The same number of angels was at her house. That's where the confusion set in. When the lieutenant didn't follow protocol, a red flag did not notify us of the probable response God would send."

SERGEANT: "Then, where was the multitude sent, General?"

(Before closing his mouth, the sergeant got a surprised look on his face).

"Oh, General, no! Don't tell me that the angels were sent to the poor little boy's country. Wow, that's terrible! How awful, and what a big deal it was for that lieutenant not to follow protocol! What happened next?"

GENERAL: "Of all the unimaginable things, God sent hundreds of angels to President Mantre's villa. Later, we got the information from a captain demon who was stationed there about what went on that night at the villa. The captain demon, whose name was

Raulk, reported later that the angels shot in like a rocket."

SERGEANT: "I hate to be around whenever those angels are gathered together in such a great number. The serious prayers bring forth the power from heaven against our cause of destruction."

GENERAL: "Demon Raulk reported that the angels were completely focused, waiting for a signal from heaven command. They were lined up in a strategic formation, eyes staring trance-like, with total obedience to God. After the whirlwind of angels arrived, they kept going into their lines and didn't say a word."

SERGEANT: "There was no talking among themselves?"

GENERAL: "No, it was very strange because they usually talk enough for a devil to know a little, or we can kind of guess what's going on in a situation. This event was different, however … no talking. Demon Raulk's report said you could sense that they were already briefed and were waiting for the signal to move. Extreme power was radiating from this troop, the kind that tells a demon that something major is about to go down. Demons were wondering what was next. Something big was going down, but the 8709th Sector could not figure out what righteous move was about to take place. The lieutenant had no idea of the foreign activity and the problems that were stemming from little Suzy and her prayers.

"Like I said earlier, when the lieutenant missed the protocol of Section 21, Paragraph 4 of the Demon Doctrine and Rules (DDR), the warning flag was not posted. That would have made sure a tracker demon was sent to keep tabs on some of the flow of prayers and their final destinations. Because the lieutenant did not follow protocol in Sector 383, the 8709th Sector was not flagged; thus, the proper block strategies were not implemented. Demons of the 8709th were scrambling to find out what to do next! Because of all the demons running around in chaos, the communications between official devils were broken down, and no one knew what the other one was doing. It was a big mess! One of the private demons, while studying events and records for the quarter that night, ran across the mistake and contacted the lieutenant. Instantly, Lieutenant Blaydor called the 8709th and was patched through to the major on station. With no sense of urgency in his voice, the lieutenant contacted a Major Tefin of the 8709th and told him about the prayer of little Suzy! He apologized for the communication breakdown at the 383rd. The lieutenant told the major there was an apparent escalation of angelic activity headed their way and that they might want to increase the troops in their area to handle any overflow of trouble. Boy was *that* an understatement! Raulk's report says the major chewed out the lieutenant like no devil's business. Needless to say, the lieutenant was demoted and sent to Satan knows where.

"Sergeant, let me tell you what happened next. The orders were passed to the angels, and the battle was on. But there were not enough demon troops to hold the ground. The angels came in a magnitude of force and kept the demons held off. They pushed the 8709th Sector defense back too far to block that attack. Raulk lost a lot of ground that night, Sergeant, a lot of ground indeed."

(General sighs, thinking about how intense the night was reported to be. Then the general continues the story.)

"Now, let me tell you more about the country of Pelomia and their devil-controlled leader and staff.

"President Mantre had a right-hand man presiding in his government cabinet, Commander Degalo Les. Commander Les's and President Mantre's association went far past the official stance of military teamwork; Les was actually considered a friend to Mantre, at least as much of a friend as someone could be considering Mantre was a self-centered, trust-no-one type of person. The relationship that these two now have is more strictly business, any business that would exalt the power of Mantre. Mantre is the most important political leader anywhere. Just ask him."

SERGEANT: "What was the plan that Mantre had for more destruction?"

GENERAL: "I'm getting there. Like I said before, Sergeant, Mantre was planning to use chemical weapons on his own people and to blame the incident on his neighboring country, Zeltonia."

SERGEANT: "We're all for destruction, General, but what else besides selfish ambition was this resident after?

GENERAL: "He was motivated by greed. *Greed!*"

SERGEANT: "What do you mean?"

GENERAL: "You see, President Mantre was testing these chemical weapons and their effects for the leader of Riamaz, President Leopold Herlo. Riamaz is a country populated by some 400 million people. President Herlo of Riamaz was paying President Mantre 100 million dollars cash to prove the chemical's destructive capabilities and how an antidote Mantre had would actually work on humans. This would give Mantre the final money he needed to complete his nuclear arsenal to invade his neighboring friends and expand the Mantre empire. Then with that much power, a devil can do a lot of destruction to the world! The funny thing was that after Mantre built his nuclear arsenal, he planned on turning on Riamaz and removing President Herlo."

SERGEANT: "Real nice, man. This guy Mantre is a real nut. Wait! Let's back up a second. Doesn't he know that the chemicals can kill him, too?"

GENERAL: "Not so. Remember that I spoke of the antidote. That's what the big money was all about. This chemical would not affect anyone who had been given a pill. Supposedly, Mantre had developed a group of chemists who had come up with an antidote for the deadly chemical, Demtruxen. This discovery would not cause any effects to the person exposed to

Demtruxen if administered two hours before exposure. The antidote can be administered in drinking water. Demtruxen dissipates after just 4 days without any apparent side effects. President Herlo wanted to see the effect for himself. Demtruxen is a wonderful chemical in the hands of the right power, a hungry selfish individual!"

SERGEANT: "I see! President Mantre is pretty sneaky!"

GENERAL: "Deadly. That's why we did not want to fail our mission to get him to gas his own people. This President is so wicked it will be easy to persuade him to do just about anything for our side in the future."

SERGEANT: "Sounds like this plan is coming together quite nicely."

GENERAL: "Let me continue; this is just the tip of the iceberg. Where was I? President Mantre was sending out Commander Les to scout out the area at the outskirts of towns and villages to see how many were going to be affected and how to set up the area for the fake skirmish. What a trip, it was only last week that Mantre had a peace summit with Zeltonia's government leader. All along, he was planning to infiltrate their intelligence to find a way to fake an attack. He would then use that lie to say he is devastated that his neighbor Zeltonia would commit such an act against Pelomia, but now Pelomia must retaliate."

SERGEANT: "Wow, this Mantre is our type of guy!"

GENERAL: "Exactly! Meanwhile, back in the States, keep in mind that little Suzy is still praying, so the demon forces are being limited. To make things worse, the little boy Suzy has been praying for lives near the small Christian mission on the outskirts of Zeltonia at the edge of Pelomia. Even though the leaders of Zeltonia are not believers in Christ, they welcomed the free missionary help for their people for food and education. The mission even brought in volunteer medical help and training for nutrition and hygiene. A man and wife team, Mark and

Lisa West, ran the mission. They were supported by a few small churches near Kansas in the USA. Also, a young man named Gary Sutton was on a summer break from high school and was helping as a volunteer. That particular morning, the missionary and his wife were praying, and—you guessed it—the little boy, Ramey, was included in their prayer. Also, at that very moment, little Ramey was praying. It was a simple little prayer until it got mixed in with little Suzy's prayer back in the States."

SERGEANT: "Oh, no! A double child faith prayer overlap! I hate those; they cause the power to be multiplied and the Spirit of God intercedes with an exact answer to the request."

GENERAL: "Angelic multitudes were pushing our soldiers to their limits. It was becoming apparent by the casualties on our side that this little Suzy's prayers were highly effective and had to be stopped. We needed to get closer to Mantre to manipulate him to step up his plan of using Demtruxen, but at that time, no strategies came to mind, even with Dark Force 5 special tactics working on the problem."

SERGEANT: "Dark Force 5 was called in?"

GENERAL: "Yes!"

SERGEANT: "Please continue; sorry for the interruption, but, wow … Dark Force 5!"

GENERAL: "Quiet! Where was I? Oh, yeah, Commander Les usually had a driver to take him around in the jungle area, but the angels caused the driver not to show up when the time came to depart, so the commander drove the Jeep to the outskirts of town on his own. It was a hot day, the sun was in his eyes, and an angel moved a tree limb down that blocked the sign for the route the commander needed to take. The road was really rough, and another angel came in and threw down a piece of metal that blew a tire of the Jeep! So, there is the commander down the path the angel caused him to take, with a flat tire, and the demons didn't have any idea what to do next!

"Wouldn't you know it, the commander was stuck in the area where the mission was located. Hot and sweaty, the commander was looking for the jack to change the tire. The angels fought hard and drew so close to the commander that we couldn't even cause him to cuss.

"The commander could not get the jack to work—it was jammed or something. The heat of the day was scorching, so he removed his gun and top shirt (the one with his rank on it) and placed them in his duffel bag.

"Out of the brush came Gary, the teenage boy who was volunteering at the mission. He slowly walked up to the Jeep and said, 'Excuse me, sir. Do you need any help?' Sergeant, the commander is usually so arrogant that he would have told that kid to go fly a kite, but there were a couple of angels around this time, and the commander looked at Gary and said, 'Yeah, maybe you can help me, especially if you have a jack on you.' Gary let out a small laugh, then he asked the commander if he could take a look at the jack. The commander handed him the jack, rolling his eyes as if to say, 'Sure, you're going to fix this when I can't?' Gary got out his knife, a piece of wire, and some loose hardware from his pocket. A few minutes went by, and Gary actually got the jack to work. The commander said, 'Very impressive!'

" Commander Les did not let Gary know who he was. He just said he was a soldier who took a wrong turn at the fork in the road a few miles back. 'Fork in the road!' Those angels were deliberately setting up this guy to meet someone to tell him about God. We are not stupid!"

SERGEANT: "General, don't tell me that the teen was able to talk to the commander about God!"

GENERAL: "Yes, for some reason—I guess it was because the boy was helping the commander change the tire—he actually was not his normal cruel, lying self. The commander assisted Gary, and they finished the job in no time at all. 'Where did you learn to help people, son?' asked the commander. 'I mean, why do you volunteer to help a stranger? What's your motive?' Gary said his motive was to 'do unto others as you would have them do unto you.' The commander asked, 'Where did you learn of this?' Gary replied, 'It is in the Bible.' "

SERGEANT: "Oh, General, this story is really sickening!"

GENERAL: "Quite, so can I get to the more important parts?"

SERGEANT: "*More* important?"

GENERAL: "Gary told the commander about the missionaries who fly into the village and bring clothes, food, and Bibles to give to the less fortunate villagers and their children. Then he told him about how God sent His Son to die on the cross for him. He told the commander that Jesus loves him. Finally, there was a break, and two demons pushed forward and quickly sent a thought to the commander to stop being so friendly with this Gary. 'He is full of bologna, commander. You need to go,' the

demon told him. The commander said, 'I hope your religion keeps you safe. Have a nice life.' With thoughts of how this boy would probably be dead in a few days from the chemical gas, the commander let out a small sinister laugh. Then he put the Jeep into gear and sped off."

SERGEANT: "General, that was a close one."

(The general puffs on his cigar.)

GENERAL: "Sergeant, this story is still going."

SERGEANT: "But our guys got in a good hit. The commander was getting back to his old self, right?"

GENERAL: "Let me tell you what happened next. You see, that darn Gary threw his Bible into the back of the Jeep, and then an angel slid it into the duffel bag. To top it all off, the angel sat on the bag the whole way back to the commander's barracks. Gary began to pray for the commander."

SERGEANT: "I hate when they do that!"

GENERAL: "Yes, when the commander got back and was unpacking his duffel bag—you guessed it—the Bible fell out. The angel flipped the pages so the book landed open, face up, to the gospel of John. The commander reached down to pick up the Bible, and one of our demons slapped the cover to cause it to close and spin on the floor. Then the fight was on. The angel knocked our demon hard against the wall and caused the Bible to open as the commander was reaching again. This time, the angel had the pages bent back to the gospel of John. More demons were dispatched, but the angel was extremely powerful. One angel was holding off 13 demons. Something big was taking place. All of a sudden, that beam of light from heaven came into the room, and you know what that means …"

SERGEANT: "Yes, it's that Holy Spirit calling the humans to receive Jesus."

GENERAL: "Exactly! Once the power is sent, it stuns the demons to a point where it's unbearable to stay around. They tried a fast retreat, but our demons were hurled against the walls and pinned there as the force of the Holy Spirit was calling the commander to receive Jesus."

SERGEANT: "I know, the demons have no power whatsoever when that free choice is being made by a human to receive God's Son, but if they reject Him, then our demon forces are free to move forward and fight for their souls to keep them in deception and eventually drag them to hell."

GENERAL: "The commander read John 3:16. 'For God so loved the world that He gave His only begotten Son, that whoever believes in Him should not perish but have everlasting life.' The commander accepted the invitation from God, and the air was thick with more angels coming into the room and rejoicing. The commander prayed, 'Lord, I am a wicked man. I have done great evil. I did not realize that You accept me after all the lies, cheating, and even murder I commit. I am so sorry for the man I have been. Forgive me, I ask. Help me, God! I accept your Son, Jesus. Amen.' "

SERGEANT: "I hate that."

GENERAL: "Yes, Sergeant, it was an awful night. The commander really went to his knees and asked God to forgive him and to give him the gift of his Son."

SERGEANT: "Sickening, absolutely sickening."

GENERAL: "Yes, absolutely. I wish we could figure a way to be able to move when God sends down His Spirit, but none of the demons in high authority and no professors have figured a way to be physically released to fight until after the human makes his free choice."

SERGEANT: "Man, I wish we could figure something out. What happened next?"

GENERAL: "Devils were then seeing the bigger picture. Little Suzy's prayer for the little boy—I believe Ramey was his name—was causing this disturbance. About that time, Dark Force 5 figured that this little Suzy's prayers for Ramey were causing God to send forth all these angels to President Mantre's area to change the whole chemical destruction plan. It was apparent that the angels were being sent to do all this battle to answer the prayer for the protection of little Ramey. Dark Force 5 promised that a plan was being put together to bring in a different angle. Demon Command told them time was running out and they had better come up with something fast or else the destruction would not be as big as planned."

SERGEANT: "Pardon me, General, do you have any more cigars?"

GENERAL: "Yes."

(He pitches the box of stogies on the table. The sergeant snatches one and lights up.)

SERGEANT: "Continue, sir."

GENERAL: (Disgusted by yet another interruption, he wondered if this demon was ever capable of keeping his mouth shut.) "Yes. Commander Les reported back to Mantre the next morning, but he was so filled with the Spirit of God that the demons could not get him to buy any thoughts of disobedience to God whatsoever. The commander walked into President Mantre's office, and Mantre began to ask him for his report about the outside villages. He wanted to proceed with his plan for the little fake skirmish in four days. Also in the room were some other government officials, about sixteen in all, and a certain general named Baltor Sealta. General Sealta hated commander Les, and he always tried to find a way to get him in trouble. Commander Les walked close to President Mantre. Our best demons were standing by, but they could only manipulate the others in the room, not the commander. He was surrounded by three angels and was glowing with the Holy Spirit."

SERGEANT: "General, that brightness always makes me nauseous. That heavy protection for those new believers is really hard to break through."

GENERAL: "Yes, devils must be patient and always be ready for the free choice to the dark side (FCDS) in order to step in. The new revisions for FCDS have not been field tested very long, Sergeant, but demon command inserted them in the DDR anyway. The revision theory is the following: The 'FCDS step-in' takes place whenever a new believer or restored backslider takes their free choice (within first hour of restoration) and ponders evil for a few seconds to accept the thought to sin. Sergeant, the commander is now a new believer and is praying sincere prayers to God for help."

SERGEANT: (Shaking his head.) "Yes, dark side steps in, but with new believers, it is so hard to accomplish."

GENERAL: "Right. That's why you need to follow Section 4, Paragraph 7 of Demon Doctrine and Rules (DDR), and I quote, 'Downfall of new believers in Christ, although extremely difficult, may be instigated by free choice dark side (FCDS) step-in but must have a sentry posted to monitor the reaction of all free choice prayers set for angelic protection, due to sentry call of action in Level 5 and or Level 6 or greater, but not to exceed the thoughts of the above-mentioned.'"

(The sergeant shakes his head as if to agree.)

GENERAL: "You don't really understand what I am saying, do you?"

SERGEANT: "Oh, yes. I guess a little clarification is in order, or maybe I will figure it out in a minute."

(The general takes a big breath, then exhales in disgust.)

GENERAL: "I am going to have to take a look at your credentials and update your folder. I am having serious doubts about your position in leadership."

SERGEANT: "Oh, there are no problems with my abilities, I assure you, General. Believe me, sir, I am ready for this promotion."

(The sergeant is sitting up straight in his chair and gets a look of concentration on his face. Then, as if a light bulb went on in his head, the sergeant speaks out, interrupting the general's story.)

"The subject of FCDS step-in … Oh, yeah, now I remember … it is always necessary to post a sentry to stand by and wait for the smallest break in angelic protection and then to send in two teams of demons. Both teams are to await orders from the sentry before any attack. First team is the blue team; they are to be standing by, waiting to influence the mind and remind the human of past failures. The second team is the red team, and their job is to sneak in with a work of the flesh thought, and try to snag the stupid human into taking the bait of temptation. Timing is critical, and if six seconds pass in a free choice dark side step-in, the sentry is to send for backup: Force 5 tactical squad. Let me think for a minute. Okay, I've got it. If Force 5 does not penetrate within 13 seconds, then the sentry contacts the Strategic Command for that sector for further instructions. There, general!"

(The sergeant leans back in his chair as if exhausted from having to recall so much tactical information.)

GENERAL: "Well, I'll be, Sergeant! Very good! That is correct. It surprises me that you really could quote procedure. FCDS step-in is a great maneuver and has brought wonderful success for our cause!"

SERGEANT: "So, what happened next, sir? What happened in Mantre's meeting?"

GENERAL: "I told you that the sentry was posted?"

SERGEANT: "Yes."

GENERAL: "There was no break, so the time limit expired and a new strategy had to be played. Strategic command sent word to take out the commander at all costs. So hatred demons, twenty-four in all, were sent into the room to constantly invoke hate thoughts in the people. It was working for us quite well, but more angels were starting to enter the right side of the room. This meant trouble! Next, the commander was asked a second time by the President to give a report about the plan to gas the people and blame Zeltonia. About this time, President Mantre was getting steamed because he did not like anyone to refuse to answer him. He hates to ask more than once. The commander spoke and said he could not be involved in the plan any longer, that killing innocent people was not right, and that he resigned from command. The room began to get very loud with all the different people talking at once. Then in a loud voice, President Mantre, said, 'Silence!' Everyone was quiet. This was the break we were hoping for. Demons with hatred thoughts were rising very high in all the people there, especially General Sealta. Everyone was silent while hatred demons were circling the left side of the room."

SERGEANT: "That's right, the left side always gives more evil power to us."

GENERAL: "Of course, the left is our power; the right is God's. Mantre walked over slowly toward the commander. You could hear the leather of his boots squeak slightly as there was total silence in the room. The President began to speak as he drew closer and closer until he was positioned directly in front of the commander, just inches from his nose. Mantre began to speak in a firm whisper to the commander, 'What is the meaning of this? How dare you undermine our operation! What reason do you have for throwing away the chance of a lifetime to be put on the map as a hero? Degalo, you will be known for saving Pelomia from that hostile Zeltonia chemical attack! A wealthy hero at that; the world will not know what happened, but I will pay you handsomely, Degalo! Innocent people? Since when do you care about people? Money and power—success is what you have always cared about. What are you thinking?'

"Mantre turned around and began slowly walking, rubbing his hand nervously back and forth over his mouth, then scrubbing his hand over his head to the back of his neck. The President stopped walking and then turned back around with a quick snap and hit his hand to his head. He said to the commander in a normal tone, 'Degalo, maybe too much strain has been on you lately. Take a couple of days off and get your head together. Yes, that's it,' said Mantre, smiling and shaking his head in approval of the decision he had made.

"Everyone in the room was watching intently. 'That is the answer here,' Mantre said. 'Take a short break.' Then Mantre walked back over to Les and came close enough to place his hand on the commander's cheek. He looked him in the eye and said, 'This mission is too important for any slip-ups; we must not fail.' He patted the commander's face lightly, then stepped one step back, looked around the room and said, 'I, President Mantre, have decided to close this meeting until two days from now. At that time, the commander will lead our strategy to chemically gas the outskirts area of the villages of Pelomia. Right, Commander Degalo?' Mantre smiles with confidence. There is silence all around. You can hear the clock on the wall ticking for seconds.

"Then the commander said, 'No, sir, I cannot be a part of this plan any longer.'

" 'What!' said Mantre, his voice louder and the veins in his neck bulging. The people were all talking at once, and the room was in turmoil as confusion-demons slid in to enhance the battle strategies.

"Then the commander spoke loud enough to be heard, 'Hold on a minute, gentlemen. I cannot be a murderer any longer.' The people were murmuring quietly, so the commander kept talking a little louder. He said, 'I have found life … a new life by accepting God's Son into my life.'

"The room was breaking out in tremendously loud conversation. Everyone in the room was stunned. The commander was a ruthless, greedy man. He never cared about anyone in his life. He had left his family years ago and never looked back. Then Mantre silenced the group by slamming his whip down on the table and said, 'What are you saying? Are you crazy all of a sudden?'

"The commander began telling the whole group about how he repented to God and asked to receive His Son. By this time, Mantre was really stunned and just stood looking extremely bewildered at his commander.

"Then General Sealta spoke up, loudly interrupting everyone, 'President Mantre, you have always said that this type of action is not to be tolerated by your government. This Christ-faith talk is for the weak-minded and must never be allowed in this organization.' Then Sealta said, 'Guards, seize this man!'

SERGEANT: "Great, this story is turning out great!"

GENERAL: "Wait a minute, Sergeant, let me share what went on next. Okay, the guards arrested the commander, and without any resistance, led him down to the prison. President Mantre was really hurt and confused that his commander was talking like a nut, or so he thought. Later, as Mantre was in his chambers alone thinking over the day's events, the greed-demons were hovering to keep up the pace in his mind. He was thinking about the millions of dollars at stake and how wealthy he would be. What is this crazy talk from the commander about God, anyway? He would be a god himself after only a little while. What is wrong with Degalo?"

SERGEANT: "What was going on at the jail, General? What tactics were being deployed on the commander to get him to doubt his decision to chuck the mission?"

GENERAL: "Very good thinking, Sergeant. You are right, the commander was a great asset to the dark side for years, and we didn't want to lose him. Back at the jail, there were demons injecting doubts and fear, trying to deceive the commander's mind, but he was praying for direction from Jesus. All the tactics we could come up with were not penetrating. Three angels were holding off the demons at the jail. The free choice the commander made was to obey God."

SERGEANT: "What a waste of a perfectly good, evil person!"

GENERAL: "Yes, I agree. Now let me tell you more. Remember, Mantre was alone in his chamber. General Sealta looked through a slightly opened door in direct contact with Mantre's room and said, 'My president, may I have a word with you?' Mantre was not very rational; he was more stunned and confused about the commander's action.

" 'Yes, come in,' said Mantre. The hatred was strong in General Sealta's heart, but he sensed that Mantre was having compassion for his friend, the commander.

"General Sealta walked over to Mantre, stood about three feet from him and said, 'My President, the mission is the most important thing at this point. The money that it brings will allow you, my President, to be a great power, a wealthy man, a powerful leader, a man to be feared, because you, my President, will own your own nuclear weapons and artillery.' He continued, 'It will all be yours, my President, all yours. No one will be able to stand in your way.' Then Sealta let a few seconds pass for Mantre to soak up what he had said. He continued, 'Power, money, leadership, all yours.'

"The greed-demons started working on Mantre's mind. 'My President, I have a solution for the dilemma that the commander caused today.'

" 'A solution?' said Mantre.

" 'Yes,' said Sealta, 'The commander's actions and speech are very dangerous to our mission. I know you and he were friends growing up, but, my President, he now does not share in your vision. His action today shows he has become mentally deranged. Something has snapped … all this talk about God.'

SERGEANT: (Interrupting one more time.) "I see what you are trying to do! You are trying to get the commander locked away by Mantre."

GENERAL: "No, we wanted to kill him. The demons were manipulating Mantre's mind, and General Sealta was being smooth in slowly sliding the thoughts to Mantre to let him take good care of his old friend. It was working very nicely. General Sealta, with sympathy in his voice said, 'My President, what is more important? You always say it is the mission; the mission is most important.' This is where hatred and a murderous demon force came to Mantre. Then General Sealta said to Mantre, 'What will your soldiers think if you let this go? You know what you must do. I am sorry it has to be this way.'

" 'What are you saying?' asked Mantre.

" 'You must set the example in front of your staff, my President, or they will think of you as a weak man, and they will not be afraid of you, my leader.' A moment of silence fills the room. Then Sealta continues, 'You must execute the commander yourself, my President, in front of your staff. It is the only way. If you do not take this matter into your own hands, your staff will lose respect, the respect you have made for yourself. The respect should not falter; it's taken years. My President, you are so mighty, and you have come so far. Please do not risk the mission and your domain of absolute power—Pelomia's leader!' Walking slowly closer, Sealta reached out and grabbed Mantre by both upper arms and pulled him to himself with a vicious grip. He was directly face to face, within inches of the now sweating face of Mantre. Then Sealta firmly, in a low demanding voice, said, 'Mantre, my President, Commander Les will ruin all you have worked for, all the time invested in the mission for which we swore to die and for which many lives have already been sacrificed.'

"Breathing heavily, Mantre said, 'But Degalo is my friend.'

"There is silence as Mantre realizes Sealta has gripped his arms. Mantre slowly looks down at Sealta's hands and then raises his eyes to directly look into Sealta's face. Mantre then quickly snaps his arms back and says, 'You dare touch me? *No one* touches me! I will have you shot!'

"Sealta is now staring into Mantre's eyes and has no idea what to expect next. Without fear, Sealta stands there quietly with compassion in his eyes. A moment of silence passes, and then

Sealta speaks, 'You see, my President, I myself even risked my life to try to snap you out of the feelings for a so-called friend who has gone crazy. The mission, the mission! Please keep your focus! The commander was a friend; now he is the enemy! Sadly, my President, your friend has turned against you and disgraced your position.'

"Mantre turned his back to Sealta, and for about two minutes, stared at the picture on the wall."

SERGEANT: "What *was* the picture on the wall, General?"

GENERAL: "The picture was of a great man who gave multitudes of demons reason to be proud. It was Joseph E. Mantre, Sr."

SERGEANT: "Oh, yeah, I remember. He was a legend of evil." (Hesitating, he continues.) "Tell me, why was Joseph, Sr., so evil?"

GENERAL: "Dufer, you must be an idiot! You don't read up enough on the generational destruction code and archives, do you?"

SERGEANT: "Please, General, give me insight on the life of Joseph, Sr."

(General Zalk rolled his eyes and took in a deep breath.)

GENERAL: "Sergeant, you really are getting on my nerves, but I will tell you!"

(The veins were expanded in the general's head. He was extremely ticked off. When he had regained a calmer disposition, he continued.)

"Joseph's past made him such a legend because, when he was twelve years old, he went to the dungeons of Bordek, taking a knife, an old worn Bible, and a kerosene lamp down with him. Joseph laid the Bible down on the filthy dungeon floor …"

SERGEANT: "Wait, I can see why he took the kerosene lamp: so he could see in the dark dungeon. And the knife: in case he had to defend himself from a varmint or snake. But, where did the old Bible figure in? I thought he was a wicked man."

GENERAL: (With disgust in his voice.) "You interrupted me again! Sergeant, you keep interrupting me! How am I ever going to finish this story?"

SERGEANT: "Sorry, I won't interrupt again. Continue, please, continue … but if …"

GENERAL: "What now, Sergeant!"

SERGEANT: (Muttering under his breath.) "Never mind. I was just wondering where the Bible came from …"

GENERAL: "Okay, I will go up one more generation for your benefit."

SERGEANT: "What are you talking about, General? What other generation?"

GENERAL: "I did not want to explain where the old Bible came from because it just causes us to have to go back a generation to the great-grandfather."

SERGEANT: "I am confused. What does he have to do with the Bible?"

(The general shakes his head back and forth and stares at the ceiling. Then he reaches for another cigar and lights up.)

GENERAL: "Sergeant, I did not want to go back in the family history any further, but I guess I have to …" (Raising his voice.) "… so I can get on with the story! Alright now, let me see, it was back in 1920 when the great-grandfather, Omar Mantre, lived. Omar's wife, Elsa, had a baby and named him Joseph E. Mantre. Omar was a wealthy man, and I am not going to go into his history except to say that he was into oil exploration. He was financially loaded. At the young age of 23, he married Elsa Holosee. The bad news is, Omar and his wife were actually church-going, born again believers. We kept close to them, sending demons to keep the temptations coming in as fast as we could, but this couple kept praying, attending church, and so on. As I said, time went by, and they had a son whom they named Joseph. This is President Mantre's father, Joseph, Sr., the one we have been talking about. Devil forces in the local Sector 795 tried to get Omar to give into temptation with hatred, contention, and greed, but Omar was already so wealthy, he did not flinch at greed. He seemed to love everyone, so hatred was out. However, 795 did notice an occasional outburst of wrath. Omar was seemingly nice and proper in public, but at home we tempted him, and he would actually yell at his wife.

"Sergeant, since *outbursts of wrath* are sins against God, that was a stronghold that we were counting on to bring this couple down. The problem was that Omar kept repenting only a little while after he sinned, so he was forgiven, thus breaking the chain of sin. Omar would sin and repent, then sin and repent again. We sure needed him to stay in those sins so we could have rights to destroy. Years went by, and finally, one morning, after analyzing Omar's records, the devils at Command 795 almost slapped themselves when they discovered what had not been tried yet; it was overlooked somehow."

SERGEANT: "What?"

GENERAL: "The easy wipeout: another woman. All that needed to be done by the demon of Sector 795 was to send a woman, a devious woman, to that church where Omar and his wife attended. 'Now it will be a cinch,' said the sector devil patrol. 'Another woman is a strong temptation.' So a new visitor, the woman of evil, named Lori, visited the church and talked to Omar and Elsa. The first morning after service, Elsa and Lori became friends, but Lori was very sneaky; she would smile at Omar only when Elsa was not looking. Those devilish smiles were getting to Omar; the demons kept telling Omar that he really needed to lust after Lori. Several months went by and Lori kept on smiling at Omar and keeping her friendship with Elsa. Lori was devil-controlled, and we were not going to give up.

Omar would sin, repent, sin, repent. God forgave him, and then we tempted again with an outburst of wrath. It's just a matter of time before we will win. Omar got upset with Elsa one night and did not repent for his outburst of wrath. Great! The demon placed the ball and chain on Omar's leg and told him, 'It's okay. You have a right to be mad and even contentious toward your wife.' Omar bought the other temptation, and another demon slapped on a second ball and chain. We knew all that needed to happen then was for Omar to go into town and see Lori; that's the next set up."

SERGEANT: "Did it happen, General?"

GENERAL: "Hold on. Let me finish. We set up the scene where Lori was sitting on a bench at the local park. She was dressed beautifully with lace and wore sweet perfume to entice. Now comes our victim. Omar thought he was just on a walk to cool off from the fight with his wife. There he is, walking down the street, unaware of the setup the devils have accomplished, and he sees Lori alone, sitting on the park bench in the cool of the night. The demons deceived Omar into thinking it was okay to stop and talk with Lori. As they talked, the demons kept planting the thought, 'You really like this woman. She understands you, and she smells so heavenly. It's okay to stay here.' Omar sat down close to Lori, too close. He had taken the bait and BAM! The demon of lust was able to slap the third ball and chain onto Omar's legs. Omar was deceived, and Lori kept on secretly meeting him. Success!"

SERGEANT: "Yes! We have a victory. Christian deceived; wonderful indeed! I should trademark that! So how did it come out?"

GENERAL: "Well, Omar and Elsa ended up divorced, so it was easy to keep young Joseph deceived into not believing in God because why would a loving God allow their family to be destroyed by divorce? As Joseph E. Mantre grew older, he despised anything to do with God. His father, Omar, gave him a Bible when he was only seven years old and signed it, "To Joseph, with love from your mother and father. We will always be a family together by the love of Jesus." However, as he was growing up, young Joseph saw the way his father yelled at his mother, and he was confused about the peace that Jesus promised. If his Dad and Mom could not even have it in their own home, was it real? Demons used the divorce to really confuse Joseph and to grow a steady and increasing hatred for his father, Omar, because he left his wife, Elsa, for Lori. Joseph saw a lot of sinning Christians, so it was easy for the devils to keep him deceived into staying lost. Yes, Joseph was turning toward the devils' side, and we sure were going to oblige him. He never did receive Jesus; that's where the dungeon story and the old Bible come in.

Now, getting back to my story … Young Joseph Mantre, Sr., went to the dungeon of Bordek, laid the Bible down, and then poured a little kerosene over it. Next, he took the knife and sliced his left hand. He humbled himself before Satan, and he knelt down before the Bible and let his blood drip onto its cover. Soon, the words 'Holy Bible' were covered with the sacrificial blood to Satan. Then Joseph set the Bible on fire. We allowed a demon to speak to Joseph and say, *'Now you belong to me forever!'* You see, Sergeant, in exchange for power and financial success, Joseph Mantre, Sr., made a pact with the devil himself to follow the ways of evil and to dedicate his generations to do the same. You see, the picture on President Mantre's wall was of his father—the wonderful devil-controlled Joseph E. Mantre, Sr., who led the people with a strong arm of violence and terror. He would kill and have his soldiers kill any who stood in his way. So as not to have to share his rule and money, Joseph, Sr., killed his own brother and then blamed it on a poor farm worker. I remember President Joseph Mantre, Sr."

SERGEANT: "Man, Joseph was a human after the heart of Satan, huh?

Please continue with the story, General."

GENERAL: "As President Mantre stared at the picture of his father, one of the many demons in the room—I believe a Level 3—went over to Mantre and spoke in a voice that sounded like that of his dead father. 'Mantre,' the demon said, 'don't let me down.'

"Mantre ran his hand over his right ear and thought, 'Am I going crazy? How can this be my father?'

"Then the demon said, 'My son, do not let me down. Sealta is right.'

"Mantre spun around quickly and had a wild look in his eyes, a stone-cold lifeless look in his eyes. Sealta had not moved from his spot all this time. Even though it had been only about three minutes, it seemed to drag on in an echo of hours.

"In almost a whisper, Mantre fastened his eyes on Sealta and said, 'Very well, let us go now. I must not let my father down.'

"Sealta had no idea what Mantre heard the demon say, so he looked bewildered, but said, 'Yes, my president, you must not let your father down.' "

"Mantre agreed to execute Commander Les and told General Sealta to go to the prison and have the guards take the commander to the outer courtyard.

"With a low, caring voice, General Sealta said to Mantre, 'As you command, my President. I will make the arrangements.' So the staff was called down to the outer courtyard. It was around dusk. The clouds were hovering low, and the sun was going down. An orange reflection from the sun shone on the staff members as they gathered, not knowing what was about to take place. Mantre arrived at the courtyard, and the staff started to question why they were called. General Sealta said in a loud, commanding voice, 'You will soon find out.'

"From out of the right courtyard door came the guards and Commander Les. Les was blindfolded. The guards stopped about fifteen feet from Mantre and the people and forced him to his knees. One of the guards ridiculed the commander, whispering to him, 'Commander, you are on your knees; maybe you should pray to President Mantre. Your God is not here.' Then the guard snickered."

SERGEANT: "It looks like Commander Les was a goner, for sure!"

GENERAL: "Yes, you would have thought so …"

SERGEANT: "What? What happened to cause any failure here? This was a sown up deal, wasn't it?"

GENERAL: "It should have been, but little Suzy was praying even more for the protection of little Ramey, and those prayers of a child are really hard to fight. Mantre looked over his staff, turned around, and walked over to Commander Les from behind. Then he stopped and said aloud for all those present to hear, 'The mission is more vital than anything or anybody.' At that, he drew his pistol from inside his jacket and cocked it. He placed the gun to the commander's head and said for emphasis, 'Nothing is more important than the mission, and nothing will stand in my way.'

"Commander Les, still on his knees and blindfolded, was praying and, with a small voice, quoted a Bible verse he had learned just that day. He said, 'Lord, forgive them, for they do not know what they are doing.' The guards were standing in a half circle, keeping the people in place while Mantre held his weapon to the commander's head. General Sealta was about twenty feet away.

"As Mantre looked up, General Sealta made eye contact with the President, intent on pushing for death, and nodded as if to say, 'Now, kill the commander.'

"It seemed that time was standing still as Mantre stood over the commander. Mantre said to the commander, 'Degalo, I am sorry, my friend, but the mission must be fulfilled.' As the people looked on with fear, Mantre's finger tightened on the trigger."

To be continued …

# EPILOGUE

This story is just an example of the battles and schemes that go on all around us all the time in the unseen world.

If you have given your heart and life to Jesus, then I urge you to be aware of every thought and temptation that comes to you. We are in a spiritual war with real adversaries.

Exercise your free choice to say no to temptation as soon as it comes. Sin has consequences. Seemingly "small" sins can sometimes have dire consequences that affect you for the rest of your life. Sin can affect not only the one sinning, but it can have far-reaching tentacles that can bring devastation to those affected by it and to future generations.

So, when temptation comes, and I assure you it will come, followed by the thought, "Go ahead; no one will ever know," remember where it's coming from and the devastation it can carry. Quickly, quickly, quickly, cry out to God for help and pray for anyone else who is involved to be set free.

Jesus gave His precious life to set us free from the sin nature. It was a very costly grace that was extended to us, so let's not treat it cheaply. Join with me in commitment to honoring our Redeemer, Jesus Christ, by giving Him our love, our loyalty, and all of our choices.

God help us all is my prayer!

# MEET THE AUTHOR

## RANDY HIGNIGHT, SR.

Randy Hignight, Sr., is a dedicated husband of over 35 years to Bobbette and father of two grown children, Randy, Jr., and Brittany. He is also the proud grandfather of two. Randy has been faithfully serving God for over 25 years. For ten of those years, he has been working on this book, a navigational tool for understanding spiritual warfare. The concepts of this book have been tested by Randy personally, and he has learned that it is really possible to live for Jesus Christ and walk as He did! *"Imitate me, just as I also imitate Christ"* (1 Corinthians 11:1). This book will also direct you to the exact Scriptures you can use to live a victorious life. If you are satisfied with your spiritual walk with God, then keep doing what you are doing. But if you want a change in your life, then experience a journey that focuses on remaining dead to sin and alive in Christ.

Randy is also a singer and songwriter. His song, *Freedom Your Freedom*, is dedicated to the families of our fallen and wounded soldiers. The CD is available at FreedomYourFreedom.com. It is also available for download at iTunes.com and Amazon.com.

www.ingramcontent.com/pod-product-compliance
Lightning Source LLC
Chambersburg PA
CBHW060133100426
42744CB00007B/766
*9781938526862*